Praise for
The Things Between Us

"In Lee Montgomery's bracing, gimlet-eyed memoir, *The Things Between Us,* news of her father's cancer is greeted with a gallon of scotch and a chaser of denial."

—*Vanity Fair*

"*Tin House* executive editor Lee Montgomery breathes new life into the dysfunctional family memoir with clean, vivid writing laced with a bitter bite. The result is *Ordinary People* meets *One True Thing.*"

—*Variety Weekend*

"Don't miss: Mumzy likes her first gin at 8:45 A.M. Big Dad loves his food, or did, before cancer took his appetite. Lee Montgomery tends to her frail, patrician parents while they cling fiercely to their habits—and, memorably, to life."

—*More* magazine

"Montgomery expertly interweaves the present-tense narration, which describes Big Dad's decline in the late 1990s, with occasional glances back to her '60s childhood, which are well placed and never gratuitous. Kudos also for her careful attention to the emotional thickets of siblinghood; she subtly renders the struggles and strains among a brother and two sisters suddenly called on to act like adults in a situation that encourages regression to childishness. The author lays bear the trials of alcoholism with a light touch, never descending into whining or acrimony. . . . Everyone with a terminally ill parent should read this spare account, which is damn near perfect."

—*Kirkus* (starred review)

"A Portland writer and editor pens a tough but bittersweet memoir of her Massachusetts WASP family brought together once again by her father's illness while also battling many demons from their past."

—*Seattle Post-Intelligencer*

"Lee Montgomery has captured the bittersweet truths of an American family with humor and grace. Much more than a memoir, the book is . . . an object lesson on how a death in the family has the power to reawaken life in others. Montgomery proves that life is far richer than fiction."

—*Metro* (New York)

"Startlingly honest and lyrically written."

—*MetroWest Daily News*

"A beautifully written book, *The Things Between Us* is the engrossing account of a family facing the loss of a loved one, which will certainly touch others in the same predicament."

—*The Oregonian*

"This isn't the familiar story of how alcoholism destroys a family. Instead, it is the story of a love affair between Montgomery's parents, one that ignores the sad realities of life and finds a way to cope not only with one partner's drinking but with the other's slow disintegration from cancer. This is a touching story about an odd family but, as you read it, you will make the family your own."

—*Wisconsin State Journal*

"Written with humor and grace, and devoid of sappy sentimentality, you laugh and you cry as you feel the family's

Praise for
The Things Between Us

"What Montgomery does, uncannily well, is to catch how normal an alcoholic family feels when you're in the midst of it. Montgomery has wrung an engrossing book from her eccentric (at best) childhood and the journey of reconnection she and her brother and sister take in the wake of their father's terminal diagnosis. . . . Montgomery's greatest gift is to be able to describe her family clearly and unsentimentally but without cruelty. That's what allows us to laugh with the Montgomerys but certainly not to laugh at them. They're much too compelling for that."
— O, The Oprah Magazine

"Most families have a black sheep. Montgomery's had a black hole—her mother, a frustrated performer and prodigious drunk. So imagine Montgomery's surprise when she is called home to mount a death watch—not for her Mumzy, but for her tight-lipped father, always something of a cipher for his children. Her memoir of a belatedly dutiful daughter, harrowing and inevitably heartbreaking, also manages to be scathingly funny." —The Boston Globe

"Damn near perfect." —Kirkus (starred review)

"This is not just another memoir of alcoholism and family dysfunction—this is the smartest, funniest, warmest, and most wicked of alcoholism and family dysfunction memoirs to come along in many years. Lee Montgomery paints flawed and aching people with a touching and lovely palette." —Anthony Swofford, author of Jarhead

"A monster mother, a beloved father, a trio of grown siblings who reunite to deal with a death in the family. The Things Between Us is unflinching and absolutely as fascinating as it is sad. It's also a scathing attack on the practice of medicine in America today and a perhaps inadvertent plea for us to rethink the role of hospice and our dying process." —Carolyn See, author of Making a Literary Life

love for each other reach through the pages of a memoir that reads like a novel."

—*Topanga Messenger*

"Montgomery's sentences and imagery are like good earth. You want to hold this stuff in your hand and your heart, because it's ultimately a journey we'll all face; our parents will get old and die, and we'll no longer be able to dodge the big questions; how do you forgive a parent who failed you? . . . Memoir done right."

—KINK-FM, *Portland Oregon*

"The simple grace of Montgomery's prose evokes a long-ago time, way before it became fashionable for autobiography to devolve into lurid semi-truths and scandal. . . . She writes with tenderness and candor, shifting smoothly into memories of past years, of the things that have come to define [her father]—and herself—as people. *The Things Between Us* is a beautiful tribute to a funny old guy who laughed loud and often, and whose daughter did the best she could to make him less lonely as he left the planet."

—*The Phoenix*

"This heartfelt memoir is a testament to the ties that bind a family—no matter how dysfunctional—together. . . . In the end, what brings them together is their shared stake in a family and a past that shaped the persons they had become. This forthright testament to the memories and emotions that inevitably bubble beneath the surface tackles universal questions of love and loss without judgment or bitterness."

—*Booklist*

"In her bittersweet memoir of her father's death from metastatic stomach cancer, Montgomery . . . skillfully shifts her narrative between the harrowing dailiness of her father's yearlong illness, her mother's escalating drunkenness, her own impending sense of loss, and a damaging familial past she recalls with deeply mixed emotions. Montgomery's lyric and nuanced rendering of her love for her miscreant tribe has comic as well as tragic moments, but she steers clear of both sentimentality and New England stoicism, creating a tender portrait of modern death and real American families."

—*Publishers Weekly*

"Montgomery writes her memoir with precision and grace, showing how a parent's decline and ultimate death can unite a family and lead to self-discovery, forgiveness, and healing."

—*Library Journal*

"An immensely heartfelt book, chronicling the slow decline and death of a beloved parent. What makes this memoir moving and memorable is that the love is firmly rooted in honesty, in a generous but still clear-sighted assessment of one family's struggles, alongside the closeness."

—Aimee Bender, author of *Willful Creatures*

"This memoir of a beloved father's dying is about resilience. What might appear as courage is instead the terrible and hilarious mechanics of a daughter's coping with both her father's failing and her outré family's inability to cope. Lee Montgomery draws the reader down a poignant, frightening, and sensual path that begins with word of her father's illness to the final separation of his sparkling spirit from his depleted body. The journey is unforgettable."

—Mary-Ann Tirone Smith, author of *Girls of Tender Age*

"Family stories are always tales of great complexity and *The Things Between Us* is no exception. Though we meet the Montgomerys—idiosyncratic, funny, dramatic, and vaguely glamorous—during the final months of Lee's father's illness, they are still entertaining to be around. The book shows us the Montgomerys, past and present, as they try to locate some kind of emotional equilibrium with this new turn of events, showing the reader that there is really only one thing between them, and that is love."

—Whitney Otto, author of *A Collection of Beauties at the Height of Their Popularity*

THE
THINGS BETWEEN US

A Memoir

Lee Montgomery

FREE PRESS

NEW YORK LONDON TORONTO SYDNEY

For Monty and Barb
and Tom

*f*P

FREE PRESS
A Division of Simon & Schuster, Inc.
1230 Avenue of the Americas
New York, NY 10020

Parts of this memoir have appeared in *AlaskaQuarterly*
and *Santa Monica Review*.

FREE PRESS and colophon are trademarks of
Simon & Schuster, Inc.

For information regarding special discounts for bulk purchases,
please contact Simon & Schuster Special Sales at
1-800-456-6798 or business@simonandschuster.com

Designed by Kyoko Watanabe

Manufactured in the United States of America

1   3   5   7   9   10   8   6   4   2

Library of Congress Cataloging-in-Publication Data is available.

ISBN-13: 978-0-7432-9263-4
ISBN-10:   0-7432-9263-4
ISBN-13: 978-1-4165-4310-7 (pbk)
ISBN-10:   1-4165-4310-4 (pbk)

CONTENTS

Contents

PREFACE

First things first. You have to meet my mother. You have to meet the Mumzy in the morning, sitting with her old tree root legs, stunted and worn, dangling off the edge of the king-size bed she shares with my father. In front of her is a purple walker, reminiscent of a racing bicycle with four wheels, its wire basket stuffed with socks, notebooks, a Kleenex or two. She looks up at the clock that sings a different bird song every hour on the hour and announces to my father, who is reading in a chair, "Monty, it is eight forty-five." She holds up three fingers to indicate the number of ounces of gin she wants in her drink. My father leaves the room, and I study my mother's face, the folds in her skin collapsed around bones and things she cannot express. I pat her shoulder and follow my father into the other room to watch him make my mother a drink—one of his many chores since Mother broke her shoulder a few years earlier.

In the kitchen an old wooden chest of my grandfather's stores booze and nuts and crackers. My father flips open the

top, reaches into its belly to pull out a half-gallon jug of Tan-
queray, and pours it into a jigger twice. There is something
disconnected about his movements, but he says nothing. The
only sounds come from the clinking of glass and ice and the
pouring of spirits.

I am following my father around my childhood home
now—watching, studying—because the doctors recently
found the reason that he has been losing weight and, in the
last few weeks, has found it difficult to swallow: He has a
tumor in his stomach. They do not know if it is malignant
or not, which is why I study him so vigilantly; I am trying
to decipher our future.

Dad reaches into the fridge and grabs a handful of fresh
mint, and from a cabinet, a few plastic straws, and stuffs the
bunch into the glass. He knows I watch him so he com-
pletes this maneuver with a self-conscious flair. "Take that!"

My father and I deliver Mother's drink and sit silently. I
lie back on the lavender carpet and stretch my back, sneak-
ing peeks at both of them. My mother, sitting on the edge
of the bed, stares out the French doors into the field and
my father goes back to his paperback thriller. The black
pancake face of their little dog, Inky, peeks out from under
the bed, and while I pat her, I pull at an odd tumor, a sac
of skin, that hangs off her neck. Mom looks at Dad and
then at me sadly, her expression asking, *Now what do we do?*
I smile at her, trying to be reassuring, as I am thinking
Dunno. Dunno. Dunno.

Three days earlier, on a bright autumn morning, Mom
and Pop call with the news.

"But the test says no cancer?" I say into the phone.
"That's good, isn't it?"

"Partly sunny, partly cloudy," Dad says. "It's the same damn thing. There's still a tumor there."

According to my father, they can't identify the tumor because "the asshole" on the other end of the scope can't get a piece of the thing to analyze. When he says this, all I can think about is the doctor. I had known his daughter in kindergarten. I remember her especially well because I had adored her mother, particularly how she made tuna sandwiches. I'd never seen anyone do anything so mundane with such care. She used Miracle Whip, not mayonnaise, and toasted the bread, cutting off the crusts, and slicing the beautiful remainder into tiny triangles.

"Please come," Mother says from the other extension.

"What is she going to do, Barbara?" my father says.

"You need support."

"I DO NOT need support."

"I do, then," she says.

"I need the kids available if I have to have surgery," my father says. "There's no point . . ."

"Fuck it," I finally say. "I'm coming."

"Jesus," my father says. "Your language is awful. You take after your mother."

"Go to hell," my mother says.

Dad says nothing, but hell is where I'm headed. I climb on a plane and fly east, back to Framingham and my parents' home.

1

LUNATICS

Framingham, Massachusetts

Of all the years I live with my parents, my mother is sober for only one. It is 1969, the year of Woodstock. The year the men first walk on the moon. For our family, it is the year Mother dresses up in miniskirts and white go-go boots and smokes Kools. She wears false eyelashes the size of carpet remnants and drinks Tab by the case. She cuts her bleached blond hair in the style that Twiggy has made popular, and brings crazy people home from the back wards of the state mental hospital where she is a volunteer.

There is a schizophrenic drummer, a millionaire paranoid depressive, and a manic-depressive from the CIA, who, comparatively speaking, is a relief. I am twelve that summer, and honing my cooking skills, so I make lunch while Mother drives to pick up the lunatics. I usually make hamburgers with Swiss cheese, sliced purple onion, sweet pickles and corn relish, and chocolate milkshakes. We serve them in the dining room on paper plates. I try to make conversation while I watch the crazy people eat. Everything about them is strange, but to my mind, crazy people are thrilling, even slightly glamorous—like my mother.

The schizophrenic drummer ate too much LSD in Vietnam. When he talks, he mumbles into his chest. The millionaire is too depressed to talk. He is fat and his eyes are scarily weird. He wears his hair in a mental-patient crew cut, his pants hang around his hips, and he shuffles along looking at the floor. But the CIA guy, who apparently lost it after hearing about a plot to kill someone he knew and even loved, is enthusiastic as hell, like a Labrador retriever. He babbles incessantly about everything. He is six feet tall, a handsome dandy who likes horses. He dresses in tweed with leather elbow patches, jodhpurs, and jodhpur boots, and talks in a faux British accent, as if he has marbles in his mouth. For a short time, these are our friends.

❧

It isn't Mother's idea to get sober. It's a decision that results from something that happened the previous year, the year of Johnny Mathis. He had recently come out with a new album, *Up Up and Away.* My mother loved to stay up all night and drink gin martinis and sing along with Johnny Mathis. She wrote down the lyrics in spiral-lined notebooks and practiced the melodies for days, recording them into a professional reel-to-reel tape recorder, pretending she was Judy Garland.

One morning after she has stayed up all night with Johnny Mathis, I find her passed out in a pool of blood in the downstairs bathroom, her eye bloody and swollen. At least that's where I think I find her, but when I try to picture my mother lying on the bathroom floor, the image dissolves. It's Jezebel the mink who throws me off. Jezebel was a gift from a neighboring mink farmer, a skinny fellow who has spindly teeth and resembles a mink himself. Her cage was in the bathroom, and I am now not sure there was enough room for both the cage and my mother on the floor. Maybe she isn't fully on the floor but curled around the toilet or I might have made it up. Maybe I find her on the living room floor. My mother's amnesiac cloud permeates me, too; life from these years remains hazy.

Though I am now unclear on physical details, at the time I am oddly excited. The drama of a real accident! Suddenly, all the chaos that has defined my world has something concrete to attach to. Her fall confirms a reality that is only occasionally acknowledged. Mother is a drunk, but a drunk who dreams about traveling with Johnny Mathis makes the truth more palatable: *At least she is glamorous.*

My father wraps her up and takes her to the emergency room at the local hospital. When they return later that morning, Mother's head is bandaged and angry voices bellow from behind the closed doors of the kitchen. It must be summer because my older brother Bob is home from college. He and Dad corner her. Get sober or we're taking you away. Where? Westborough State Hospital. An incredible insult. An undeniable kick in the teeth. We all know anybody who is anybody would be packed off to McLean's, where it was rumored the real rich paid more than $1000 a day. We aren't the real rich. We are the *once sort of* rich a long time ago, which, according to Mother, is better.

My mother corroborates my version of the event, referring to it for years as the time she went up, up and away in Johnny's beautiful balloon and crashed. She laughs as she says it. My father laughs, too. Ha! He laughs! She laughs! I laugh with them. My older sister, Lael, shakes her head and says, "Oh, brother." Bob screws up his face and says, "Jesus Christ."

There is a saying that my father begins to use around this time: "For Christ's sakes, Barbara, do you have to be such a horse's ass?"

And Mother? What does she say? "You tell 'em horse shit, you've been on the road."

Besides our new friends and the miniskirts, at first everything stays the same. Dad, still an engineer salesman with the cumbersome title of "manufacturers representative," spends his days driving up and down Route 128, selling widgets to the aerospace industry. Lael, only twenty-one, married a Navy ensign the year before and is living on a Navy base in Athens, Georgia. Bob is in his second year at the Rhode Island School of Design, which leaves me, the youngest at twelve, home, alone, riding my pony Happy Birthday around in circles, watching this mysterious woman who claims to be my mother click around in go-go boots towing a band of loonies.

We work hard to make it work. We walk on eggshells. We hold our breath waiting for the other shoe to drop. In the meantime, I spend the year pretending I have a mother who is normal—*sort of.* She begins to do mother-like things. We spend afternoons picking blueberries. We bake Jordan Marsh muffins and pies with recipes with secret ingredients for flakey piecrusts given to us by our neighbor. We chase Johnny Mathis, me following Mother as she tries to get backstage under a big circus tent next to the first mall in America, Shoppers' World, in Framingham, the town we live in. Mother knits cabled sweaters at startling speeds. We take a plane to see my sister in Georgia. We ride together. My parents take photographs. Mother buys me a fancy Steuben saddle and shows me how to braid my pony's mane and tail with a needle and thread. All these events seem mundane, normal, like life in an all-American family.

The balloon crash is the only time I remember my father taking a visible stand against Mother's drinking. Before this year, and after it too, my father silently endures, assuming both parenting roles. He takes me shopping for school clothes and party shoes, ferries me to and from dancing school, and watches me in recitals and class plays. Outside of that year, Mother has the dubious distinction of missing every event of my life, including graduations and my wedding.

So, I'll always be grateful to Johnny Mathis and his balloon. Nineteen sixty-nine is the sole year I look at my mother and feel something like pride. She is beautiful. She wears long dungaree coats, safari suits, and stylish straw hats. But like all good things, it is short-lived. By the summer of 1970, the lights go out again.

2

THE GARDEN

October 1998
Framingham, Massachusetts

One morning, soon after I arrive, Pops and I begin our day of chores by placing salt marsh hay around the raspberry patch. Salt marsh hay is a new idea. Past years it's been mulched leaves, but today Pops doesn't have the energy.

"My get up and go got up and went," he laughs. He holds a Winston between his lips and stomps the hay down with a foot.

In the last year, my father has grown thin. His skin is the color of ash, and he has begun to act tired, like an old man.

"Hey," he says. "This looks like it will work pretty good."

I pull a few tiers from the bale and move around the back of the raspberry patch shaking the hay apart. It's old and wet, so the center is bluish white with mildew, but I like the smell and its moist warmth and examine it closely. I had always imagined salt marsh hay would be different from alfalfa, and though it's true that salt marsh strands are longer and finer, the mix of colors—burnt brown, gold, and green—is the same. Salt marsh hay always sounded exotic, but does so especially now, because I have spent more than a decade in Southern California, far away from my New England roots. Wandering around now with my father, I cherish our traditions—mulching the garden, the making of *whatdayacallits* and *thingamajigs*—as much as I cherish the flattened As of his Boston accent and his mother's family's recipes for biscuits and plum pudding sliced with a thread.

All around the garden are Dad's handmade contraptions. Small, wooden platforms shaped like satellites hold the melons away from the earth. Half-moon domes of chicken wire, *Peter Rabbit Keeper-Outers,* shelter rows of lettuce from the rabbits and deer. An enormous walk-in chicken wire cage discourages the crows from pigging the blueberries. At the back of the garden, the acorn squash lies in wooden cradles on a sheet of black plastic that keeps the weeds from growing.

"What are those?" I point to some small pieces of wood.

"Those?!" Dad says, delighted I've asked. "Those are me squash picker-uppers." He leans down and picks up a circular plywood platform with legs and hands it to me.

I study my father's handiwork and smile. He's a classic Yankee, digging in the dirt and building ingenious devices to master small environmental challenges, to assure a grand harvest, and to pass the time.

We return to our work and when we do, I explore every part of him, trying to gauge the depth of his exhaustion, searching for any indication of the tumor in the top of his stomach.

"The size of a rabbit?" I suggest holding my hands out

to indicate a size. I then make them smaller. "A squirrel? Two cardinals?"

He does not laugh but gazes out over the back field, blowing dragon plumes of cigarette smoke, and wiggling his fingers, two of them cut off at the ends by a snow blower.

We work quietly and when all the earth around the raspberry plants is covered, we move on to the asparagus, carefully laying out their new bed, and then back to the raspberries again. He pulls a few berries from the branches, and I follow. We place them into our mouths where they melt.

∞

After lunch, we pull the dahlias and morning glories from their netting, place the huge tangled vines in the garden cart, and haul them through the garden gate down to the back of the field. A bay gelding and a Shetland pony follow us. Dad walks beside me as I pull the cart, and though we are silent, we are aware of our new roles. He has been the cart puller for all of time; him always the stronger of the two, but each year he has grown smaller. His dungaree shorts and his Lands End polo shirts fold around him now like loose skin.

"What the hell did you kids do with the other cart?" He turns; smiles, and I see our old cart in my mind, the Mercedes-Benz of wheelbarrows, light spearmint green, a four-wheeler instead of the traditional one-wheeler that often tipped.

"Ruined it hauling rocks," Pop says, answering his own question.

"Rocks? Yes," I say, remembering the grinding of a broken bearing and the oh-shit-my-father-will-kill-me sinking feeling.

"Messed with the bearing, I guess," he says.

"Yep," I say.

"Never did work after that," my father smiles, and I brace myself for what's coming.

"And then of course, you put kerosene in that car . . ."

"The Heavy Chevy," I add, finishing his sentence. "And my dear father, it ran!"

He hoots, a sweet combination of a laugh and a *humph!*

"The damnedest thing," he says. "I never understood it."

"And you, old Daddy-o, you put your fingers in the snow blower and chopped them off."

He holds them up for me—the index and middle finger are shorter than the others. "That was pretty dumb, wasn't it?"

"Sometimes, Dad, I don't think you're so bright." I poke him in the ribs with a finger.

He hoots again. This is what he told me as a girl when I did dumb things, which, according to him, bordered on plenty.

At the bottom of the field, the post-and-rail fence ends, opening to a three-tiered wire fence that separates a meadow from the woods. Somewhere directly behind the fence a defunct well remains buried. When I was a child, I loved to dig away the moss and the grass and pull up the rotten boards to see the stinky water, and though I have the same urge now, I don't start digging. Everything has changed in the twenty years I've been gone. All the old markers have disappeared and, under the new growth, I no longer know where to look.

We pull the vines from the cart and throw them over the fence in a tangled pile, far enough away so the horses can't eat them and get sick. Pop stops to rest and turns to look at the back of the house and barn, monuments to his hard work over the past forty-five years: the red clapboards and white trim of the house, the ash-colored shingles of a century-old cow barn that stands three stories tall. The crest of the barn's roof is dotted with lightning rods, their twisted steel cables fall to the ground like giants' braids.

In the distance, Mother's bleached-blond head bobs out of the glass doors that lead to a large wooden deck and a pool. She wears her Vermont Country Store white cotton bloomers, droopy at the crotch, and the Mount Hood T-shirt I bought her at the Portland, Oregon, airport. She leaves her high-tech purple walker, hobbles down the steps into the steaming turquoise water that is kept at ninety-four degrees so she can swim despite a broken shoulder and pelvis, which never fully healed. Stoyan, her twenty-five-year-old caretaker from Bulgaria, follows, carrying a tumbler of martinis that he places at pool's edge. A clarinetist, Stoyan, or The Kid as my father calls him, plays jazz in Boston by night and works for my mother during the day—making drinks and escorting her to and from the pool. It is 1:30 or 2:00 in the afternoon and this is the *Pooltini*. Mother's first drink of the day, the one my father made earlier at 8:45, was the *Gin Minty:* a tall glass of gin with a fistful of fresh homegrown mint stuffed alongside her signature red-and-white striped straw.

∞

My father's illness is our, his children's, worst nightmare.

We are friendly but far-flung, strewn across the world, making parental caretaking difficult at best. I have just moved to Oregon with my husband Tom after twelve years in Los Angeles. Lael and her husband, Jon, live in San Diego. Bob and his wife, Susan, live in the North End of Boston. An engineer, Bob often works abroad, and Susan works around the clock as a partner in a fancy law firm. None of us has children. And if asked, I don't know that anyone would know offhand how long it's been since we've shared a family meal or a holiday. Fifteen years? A family vacation? More than thirty. I visit from the West Coast once a year. Lael isn't much better. And even though Bob and Susan live in Boston, they pop by for quick visits on Thanksgiving and Christmas Eves on their way to Susan's family's festivities in Connecticut. It's not what we want, but it's what has come to be.

Now that I am here, I remember why. Mother is distant. She wanders the house, frightened, uncomfortable in her skin. She pushes her buggy with her Gin Minty precariously balanced on the ledge. Stoyan follows carrying towels. They swim. They nap. They lunch. In the late afternoons, I hear them play music together in the far room we call the Pine Room. Stoyan plays Mother's crazy piano or his clarinet as she sings along: *Zippity Doo Dah, Zippity Ay . . .*

Bobby and Susan are in Italy on vacation, due home in a few days. But I call Lael obsessively four times a day, even though I know we can only really talk at night when we can be sure Mother sleeps and is not eavesdropping. One evening, when Mom and Dad begin to doze off, I call Lael from the upstairs bedroom. I hang out the window to smoke a cigarette, and as we talk, I imagine her wandering around her kitchen, cooking dinner, picking leaves off her African violets. She is the only person I know besides my mother's mother, Grandmother Begole, who doesn't kill them.

"She is druuuuuunk," I say.

"Shit," Lael says.

We are silent, but breathe together for a while.

"Blotto. Out of it. Gonzo. Plastered."

There are clicks on the phone and I'm thinking Mother has picked up the extension.

On the floor. Out of her mind, Under the table.

"Mum?"

"Hi Mother," Lael says.

"Hi Mother," I say.

"Should I come?" Lael asks.

No one says anything. We all just hang on the phone and breathe.

The next morning, Mother and I swim in the cool morning as the sun hangs in the center of a brilliant blue umbrella sky, illuminating the pink petals on her bathing cap and her large blue eyes, stony and stunned.

"Knockers up," she says.

She sits on the steps in the turquoise blue and deeply draws her Minty from a straw. "Knockers up," she says again, lifting herself while trying to swallow. "You bet your bippy." I laugh. Why the women in my family continue to quote from the television show *Rowan and Martin's Laugh-In* almost thirty years later is beyond me, but we do. We not only bet our bippies, but also use the elegant malapropisms of my mother's mother, Grandmother Begole: we get our legs in the door, and watch *Away with the Breeze* instead of *Gone with the Wind.*

Mother stretches out and begins to swim sideways, her strong arm in motion, the other limp. She confides something daring and hopeful: She wants to pee in the pool.

"Go ahead, Mumzydoo," I say. "Pee!"

But she can't do it, and this becomes another sad thing.

As I watch my mother swim, I remember a story about an old neighbor who placed a secret dye in his pool to detect any pissers. The chemical reacted with urine so that streams of red would issue from between the legs of offending parties. This is one of my father's stories from long ago. I can still see the shift in his shoulders as he hunkered down in his favorite leather wingback chair, fiddling with something in his hands, to tell me more about this eccentric neighbor who drove around town in an antique Rolls Royce. In the foreground, Mother continues to swim, still complaining that she doesn't have the courage to pee in her own pool and though I can hear her, I am distant, spinning through time and memories of my father. I land on a bright Saturday morning where I see myself as a nine-year-old girl with my father, a forty-five-year-old man; we are digging fence postholes in the field below. My arms feel the weight of lifting and plunging the long wooden-handled cupped blades into the earth, the exhaustion and sound when we hit another rock. My father stands over me holding the crowbar ready to pry the hidden rocks free of the earth.

I was ten and eleven, respectively, when Lael and Bob left for college. During those days, in addition to drinking gin, Mother's life was about saving horses. Both activities began at seven A.M., early enough that by the time I came home from school in the afternoon, Mother was usually bombed and on the phone. The phone was dirty and red, and hung on the wall in the corner of the dining room, its short cord making it impossible to sit anywhere comfortably while talking on it. Most afternoons, I found Mother cradling the receiver between her cheek and shoulder, the cord pulled tight, sitting in a Revolutionary War era Windsor chair with broken spindles. She sat at the end of the dining room, smoking menthol cigarettes, drinking gin out of a flower vase through a gaggle of plastic straws. She was surrounded by cardboard boxes on the table and floor, boxes that were full of her paraphernalia: correspondence and fan mail; newspaper stories and photographs of her dressed up in jodhpurs and riding jackets, galloping around on a horse; her research articles about respiratory problems in horses, and the horse feed called New Hope that she developed to cure emphysema (called heaves) in horses; and a professional quality reel-to-reel tape recorder, which she would talk or sing into.

My father and I spend our lives together doing chores. We dig in the earth and move mountains of horse manure. We plant postholes for post-and-rail fences. We pull wood across fields. We play goofy rhyme games, spending Saturday mornings mastering projects and running errands.

What's your name?

Puddintane.

Where do you live?

Down the lane.

Throughout our lives, we rarely talk about Mother, but rather move around the topic silently, building dining room tables out of found wood, spending our winter months constructing tongue-and-groove stalls. I don't know that we consciously avoid the discussion as much as there isn't a lot we can say to change anything. We reserve the conversations about what to do about Mother to Johnny Mathis–like emergencies only: when we find her on the bathroom floor, or when she falls off of balconies, or when she threatens to off herself. In those days we assemble around the dining room table. Lael and Dad do the talking, but go in circles and ultimately land in the same place. According to Dad, we cannot commit her to a mental hospital because you need a doctor's signature and her doctor will not sign. But I don't know that he ever asked. Instead, we wait for things to improve, and they do, until they don't. Again. And around and around we go until the next time.

When I grow up and move away, Dad and I stay connected by conducting our projects on the phone. We repair chairs, hang window frames, plant tomatoes and corn, roof barns, wire phones and electricity, remove banisters, and install French doors with thousands of miles of distance between us. We engineer projects into eternity, and while we work together over the phone, my father hoots and *humphs* as he shares tricks of the trade.

One afternoon, soon after I arrive that October, Pop and I sit in my parents' bedroom, me on the arm of his easy chair, and plan the door for the cellar bulkhead my husband Tom and I will build for our new home in Portland. "It's not hard," he says. "The challenge, I think, Lee, is sinking those holes."

I smile, trying to visualize exactly what he is saying.

"Holes? Where? In the side of the cement?" I ask.

He smirks and takes a breath as if to say, *exactly how is it that you could be so dumb?*

I walk outside following a path of sky-colored slate stones to the bulkhead my father built forty years before and study his strategy. There is a damp, musty smell of autumn and, to my right, the lawn of the side yard is still fertile. I spent an afternoon on that lawn as a child watching my father's mother—at seventy—crawl in circles under the lilac, patiently poking through blades of grass with a finger, hunting for four-leaf clovers.

I measure the boards, drawing a picture of the door's framework, and then go back in to my place on the arm of my father's easy chair. He tells me about the beauty of lag bolts and insists that I will need a bore. I know nothing of lag bolts and bores, so he draws me a picture. We do this, drawing pictures of boards—one-by-fours, two-by-tens, and the little quarter-by-quarter boards that will help the water stream down and away. My father, a lefty, draws with his hand bent in the shape of a horseshoe above the page.

I am thickheaded when it comes to spatial decisions and I do not understand this concept of boring a hole, nor the benefit of a lag bolt, so my father says, "Come on, kid," groaning a little as he pushes the footrest of his easy chair to the floor.

We walk though the breezeway and into the barn, down the hollow wooden steps, to another door that leads into the stable and its walls of stone, past smells of hay, to another door that leads to his workshop, where his lovely stubby fingers pluck a fat bolt with a shiny knob from a drawer full of such things.

"This is a lag bolt," he says holding it out in the palm of his hand. I take it between my fingers and examine it.

"It needs a jacket," he continues, taking it back and turning it around in his hand. "You drill the hole, put in the jacket, and then screw in the bolt."

I listen to his breath, cherishing each inhalation and exhalation, and the smell of him, of cigarettes in hard red boxes and Old Spice.

"That's what it is. And that there—" He points to a short two-by-four with different-size drill bits and bores standing at organized attention. "—is a bore . . ."

Everything about my father is now tired and sad, but here in his magnificent shop with its old stone wall foundation, its shelves packed with drawers and small containers full of materials to feed, fix, fertilize, build, repair, and grow, here are the things that have shaped him. And me.

3

FURY

1965
Framingham, Massachusetts

Have you ever heard of the television horse named Fury?

Well?

Before I go any further, I have to tell you about Fury.

My mother saved the television horse named Fury. That makes me the daughter of the woman who saved Fury; our family, the family of the woman who saved Fury. In the late fifties and early sixties, Fury has his own television show and is prettier and more famous than Black Beauty. Fury, who lives on a ranch in Southern California, has emphysema. His owner, a guy named Ralph, calls my mother to ask about her research and her horse feed.

California time is different than Boston time and while my father works I watch my mother spend her afternoons on the phone. What she says during these conversations, I don't remember. But I remember her laugh, and how it always seemed to go on for too long.

Anyway, at one point, Ralph wants Mom to come to California for a visit, but my mother doesn't like to travel further than the dining room chair. He's planning on sending a private jet to the Hanscom Air Force Base to pick her up. He and Fury live out in Hollywood, you know.

Ralph isn't the only person Mother talks to about horses' breathing problems. As she says, "People call me from all over the country." They write letters, too. Boxes of them. Because my mother, a crazy, drunk housewife, is considered an expert.

Here's how it happened: Sometime in the late fifties, before I was born, the Millwood Hunt Club up the road is killing horses because of their breathing problems. Mother reads an article and gets this hunch that this respiratory illness in horses has something to do with allergies. So, she takes the horses before they are shot and walks them the few miles from the hunt club to our stable. She then consults allergists in Boston, creates a research foundation, and messes around with their feed, removing ingredients like oats and hay. She writes articles for horse magazines and all the newspapers come to take pictures of her and the horses. And if the newspapers don't come, she hires professional photographers to take pictures of her: mixing grain and molasses in the kitchen sink, feeding the horses in the barn, and standing in the field with a stethoscope. I appear in some of the photographs, screaming in her arms or standing in the background wearing little smock dresses with beautiful knit booties climbing around burlap bags full of grain in the barn. I don't remember much from this time, but I can string together stories from the photographs I find in the cellar and upstairs in the barn. What I do remember is the whine of the backdoor opening and closing as people come and go. There are women who dress in riding outfits with knee-high black leather boots with patent leather tops and spurs. There are people who wear rags and drive Rolls Royces and fancy MGs. There is a minister from a church that is missing its steeple. There is the white-outfitted, white-haired, white-skinned guy who drives the milk truck and looks like a walking glass of milk. The Entenmanns's bakery deliveryman who looks like a devil dog. The psychotics and depressives that Mother took in during her sober year are small potatoes compared to some of these guys.

The years run together but in fact there are two distinct times: pre-sobriety during the sixties and post-sobriety during the seventies. When I am small, there seem to be a lot of people we don't know. God knows how they find us, but they do. Mumzy and I spend some afternoons watching perfect strangers stop to pat the horses and then knock on the door. I let them in, and begin the grand tour in the kitchen with the bulletin board, which makes up two walls of thumbtacked newspaper clippings and family Polaroids of horses and skunks and friends, Mother in her gold lamé bikini, motorcycles, MGs, Mom and her father, Grandpa Begole, both wearing blond wigs. And I happily become the smallest assistant in the world's greatest unknown circus act as Mother pulls out her boxes of tricks: the pet mink, the horses, and the articles about heaves research, about saving the mink from slaughter, the story about being cover girl for *Feedbag* magazine; the singing, the concerto, the stories of Billie Holiday's trumpet player in Greenwich Village and of Yale Drama School. It is dramatic and exciting, a Hollywood musical gone off the tracks: Anne Sexton meets Julie

Andrews. *Long Day's Journey into Night* meets *Mary Poppins, The Sound of Music,* and *All About Eve.*

Later, post sobriety, the characters, some strangers, some old friends, grow more colorful. There is a famous doctor and a mink farmer. The maid next door who smokes Pall Malls and has brown teeth. Crazy Jane, the psychiatrist who supervised Mother's work at Westborough State Hospital, who also diagnoses psychiatric disorders in horses and drives a gold Buick she calls the golden dildo. There is Bud, a friend of my father's from college, now a traveling salesman, who likes to dance and flirt with Mother. There is the little brother of a druggie friend of Bob's, Christopher, a pathologist's assistant only a few years older than me who attends the Sudbury Valley School, a private "free" school, down the road. Christopher likes to drink with the old ladies and drives around town in a hearse.

During these years, people seem to smell a party from miles away and they show up one after the other, packing cars into the driveway, pulling them up on the lawn. Sometimes when Dad arrives home from work, he finds a large group of drunken people sitting around the dining room table, everyone clearing a spot at the head of the table for him. I am happy because I get to steal everyone's cigarettes and flirt with Christopher, the hearse-driving boy who will grow up to be an alcoholic undertaker.

On the days when strangers don't come to the door and the phone doesn't ring, Mother sits at the table smoking and watches out the window. She often dresses in her jodhpurs and jodhpur boots, and her long dungaree jacket, its pockets filled with sugar lumps. She waits for unsuspecting strangers who stop at the paddock fence to pat the horses.

When people stop, which they invariably do, Mother sometimes saunters out and says: Have you ever heard of the television horse named Fury? Well, I saved the television horse named Fury. People think she's like Snow White because all the horses whinny and run to her from all the corners of the field. They grumble and nuzzle and follow her around. People think it's magic, but I know the truth; it's the sugar lumps. Pop knows too, but the man is blinded by love and good intentions.

"I wonder what the problem is with your mother?" he says.

"Hey, Pop, no good deed goes unpunished," I tell him. "The road to hell is paved with good intentions."

We could be any number of places when he asks me this question, in any number of years.

"I wonder what the problem is with your mother?"

"Dad, I think they call it an alcoholic," I say.

"Really?" he says, as if surprised.

We could be stepping over Mom splayed on the dining room floor where she has fainted, placing herself strategically between the kitchen and table during a holiday meal. Most likely, she has passed out in some major movie star kind of way, a hand on her forehead, a gasp, and her legs folding beneath her. Whenever it is, I am trained like an EMT, and run into the kitchen and pull the ammonia from underneath the kitchen sink, soak a rag, put it under her nose and she rouses.

In later years, on the rare occasions when we still visit, we may be outside in the barn after being kicked out of the house, confused as to how the afternoon disintegrated so quickly.

Pop has his troubled look. He smiles sadly, shifts his shoulders. "I wonder what the problem is with your mother?"

Well?

I study Bob one afternoon after Mother has insisted we all leave: I am probably in my early thirties, Bob is about forty. By then, Lael has already moved to California. Bob sits in the backseat of our grandfather Begole's car, an Oldsmobile he and Susan inherited after Grandpa died. We used to call it the urine mobile because in his later years, Grandpa was incontinent. Cleaned up now, the car is parked on the front lawn under a maple tree Dad planted as a sapling thirty years before. Even middle-aged, Bob still looks like a boy half-asleep, in his Hopalong Cassidy costume. He stares out the window mindlessly patting his big orange cat that sits purring on his lap. (The cat traveled everywhere with Bob and Susan.) I don't remember where Susan is at the time, but I imagine she is close by intensely focused on a magazine.

"Bob," she might say, barely looking up from the magazine. "Let's go."

A few minutes later, she tries again.

"Bob?"

Bob seems sad, even though he has told me he doesn't care. That afternoon we end up eating hot fudge sundaes at Cape Cod Ice Cream in Framingham Center. Maybe we talk about Mother, or maybe about Dad, but most likely we don't because it is impossible to know what to say. After decades of it, we have said pretty much everything. Now all we can do is shake our heads.

My father often blamed it on the Begoles. The women, whether testy or drunk, were a particular problem. Both of

Mother's parents' families, the Hargraves and the Begoles, lived in Marquette, Michigan, a lumber and mining town on Lake Michigan, and passed down to Mother and to us their *je ne sais quois*—in and out of mental institutions, squandering fortunes, dying drunk in jail. There was a governor, a town physician, and a mayor. They were a family of considerable privilege; entitlement reigned supreme. Grandpa Begole was full of stories of going around the world in 1914, trying to sneak over walls into Swiss boarding schools. There are also stories about inventing carburetors and pistons, the family founding and losing General Motors. All the stories are about loss, and eventually I come to think of the Begoles as a family that loses things: fortunes, patents, opportunities, and minds.

For many years, Lael seems unaffected by it all, flying in and out of the back door on quick visits, driving shiny fast cars with handsome rich men. She is as zany and beautiful as my mother, and for a time, when I am still small, it seems to me that she holds all of what Mother had promised, the life we were all meant to live, a life of charm, splendor, and grace. And once upon a time, I observe with sadness and longing how smitten Dad seems with all that is possible in his eldest daughter, and as we all watch Lael grow into this bright glowing thing, Mom, Bob, and I fold inward, collapsing into ourselves, tight and dense like dying stars, each of us growing fainter and more distant still.

4

WANDERINGS

October 1998
Framingham, Massachusetts

One morning when I cannot find my father anywhere, I swing open the back door with a slam and run through the barn, past antique MG cars he restored, down the stairs, through the stable and a paddock to his garden, to the place I know he'll be. I stop at the fence and watch him standing in the center, in between the vegetables and berries, staring at the flowers—dahlias and zinnias of every variety, portulaca, and the faded peonies.

"Aren't they pretty?" he asks. It is sunny but brisk. He bends down to finger a tubular petal of a dahlia and then walks over to the zinnias and looks at them sadly.

"Now the zinnias didn't do so hot this year," he says, reaching in his pocket for a smoke. He hands me one and strikes a match. "Don't know why. It's a mystery."

I climb through the fence, and we smoke and admire the earth's work, savoring its fruits and colors while following the cloudy hot trails of the cigarette smoke moving in and out of our lungs.

The sound of a car approaches and I, like in the old days, automatically watch for a friend, but the car drives past our house. In the corner of the paddock by the road, I notice my apple tree, the last of the three saved for us kids from an old orchard.

"Do you remember those, Dad?" I ask, pointing.

"Yep," he says.

"Mine's the only one standing," I remind him, as if it is significant.

"The horses got into the others, Lee, and got drunk on the apples. Made them sick as hell. I had to cut them down."

I study my apple tree, old and crooked, and don't see any remnant of the tree house Dad built for me the summer I was nine. I can remember every inch of those boards, and the way they hooked into the tree, and how Dad sweated on a ladder wearing a brown, white, and tan print shirt. Beneath him my pony, Happy Birthday, nibbled Dad's back pockets looking for an apple or a lump of sugar.

We walk back to the garden.

"This whole garden was your idea," my father reminds me again. "Do you remember that?"

"Yep," I say, "I remember everything but refusing to help."

"You didn't," he says.

"I know," I say.

"Didn't lift a finger, in fact," he says reaching down to pull a weed.

I laugh. "How did you ever put up with me?"

"Ha!" he hoots. "Sometimes Lee . . ." He begins to say something and thinks better of it.

"I must have been god-awful."

"You weren't so bad," he says. "You just knew everything." He laughs, and I slug him in the arm.

The garden was my idea during my first year of college, but I wanted an *organic* garden like Bob and Sue's, a decision we argued about for several years until I finally gave up.

"When you plant your own garden, you can have an organic garden and watch it get eaten by them varmints."

A decade later, I did just that, with Dad on the other end of the phone patiently trying to advise me.

"I don't know what to tell you, kid," he said in response to my long, sad tales of gophers who fearlessly sucked tomatoes, peppers, and baby lettuce into the earth before my very eyes.

"If you don't get 'em, they'll get you," he said, launching into a story about a rabbit that pigs his blueberries and vegetables, and how the horse and pony work as a tag team to raid the lettuce.

"Dad, what you need is a Mr. McGregor."

"I am Mr. McGregor. Ha! And what you need are some traps. Why don't you climb in the car, go down to the hardware store, and get yourself some traps?"

But I refuse because I can't stand the idea of killing little animals.

"Suit yourself then, kid, but quit your bellyaching."

In a few days, the hometown doctors at the MetroWest Medical Center, the site made famous by the Framingham Heart Study, will snake another endoscope that contains a light and a tissue chopper into my father's throat to try to pull tissue from the tumor and other areas of his esophagus. Although the tumor has been located via a CAT scan, they have yet to get a good sample to biopsy, which is necessary for a diagnosis. Because we haven't yet learned about a high protein marker in his blood, indicating that the chances are slim he has anything but the most deadly of cancers, we can still float on hope.

In his seventy-seven years, my father has rarely been sick and has never felt the hard sterility of a hospital bed. His mother lived to one month shy of her one-hundredth birthday and his seventy-two-year-old father, an untreated diabetic, died of a heart attack in his favorite chair on a Saturday morning. I was only six when he died, and I was terrified my father would meet the same end. During dinners, I watched him very closely to make sure he didn't fall over and die.

In those days, he drank too much and ate quickly. He devoured steak and potatoes and often had long coughing fits after swallowing wrong. Many evenings, surrounded by wallpaper printed with hunting horses and lit by the street-light outside the window, I watched him cough and choke. As my mother yelled (*Monty, for Christ's sake!*) from the other end of the table, I—anywhere in age from ten to seventeen—would jump from my chair to pound him on the back, his face growing red and contorted.

I was haunted by the possibility of my father's death long before it happened. Yet, as the years clicked by and he did not meet my grandfather's end, I was lulled into a strange sense of security. Throughout my twenties and thirties, I smoked cigarettes by the cartload and cheerfully filled out doctors' questionnaires about heart disease and cancer, happily placing bold checks in the "No" column, convinced that what we said was true—Montgomerys were little and low to the ground, but tough. As Dad said on occasion, *Feel damn near perfect, gonna go damn near forever.*

When Dad began to throw up that summer before he was diagnosed, he told me that he hid in the upstairs bath so Mother couldn't hear him gag. I imagined him running up the stairs, bending his body over the sink, as his dinner came up backwards: green beans, filet of sole, a corner of bread, a string of something or another.

In between heaves, he might have caught glimpses of his reflection in the mirror, the screws in its corners hidden by tiny plastic stars. Above the two sinks with their strange gray speckled linoleum, his face would be reddening from strain. Behind him he'd glimpse the cabinet doors he assembled forty years ago, their original black iron knobs still in place.

There is an irony to this stomach-eating tumor—because for many years, Dad was a fatty. He was so fat we called him BD for Big Dad. So fat, there are very few records of it because one day—after he was diagnosed with diabetes in the late seventies, which inspired Mother to stop drinking and Dad to shed one hundred pounds—they burned the evidence.

They spent the morning padding through the house, pulling cardboard boxes of pictures from all corners, collecting it all. They found boxes in the attic behind the stone statue of an owl, behind the hanging plastic wardrobe, the blueprints for the house renovation of 1955. They found them downstairs in the cellar stuffed into file folders and cabinets, boxes and half-made photo albums under the stairs. After everything was assembled, they sat in front of the fireplace, intent on destroying all evidence of Fat Dad. They spent the day flipping Fatty into the fire, watching image after image burn.

"I tried to save a few," Mother told me over the phone one day.

I wanted to ask: *Don't you wish we could erase those years for you, too?*

During the next week as we wait for the results of the second biopsy, we still have time to pretend all is well. We wander. We shop. We garden. We nap. We drive. One day we power up one of the old MGs, the 1962 red Mark II roadster MGA. It's a sure bet for instant cheer—climbing down into the hollow shiny red convertible, pulling out the choke and the starter button and cruising in reverse out of the belly of the barn. The deep purr of the engine climbs and falls like a motor boat, the tires *whop* and *whir* as they move over the wooden boards and out onto the steep driveway. We drive along the roads of Framingham, our heads dappled in light and shadow, the leaves forming a canopy overhead.

In the distance, past rolling fields and rubbled stone walls, the trees burst in glorious regalia: cranberry and rust and yellow and orange. We pass the old Stephens house, then the fields where my mother and I rode in foxhunts. I look at my father as he drives. His hands rest on the wooden steering wheel, the Greek fishing hat that I bought the Christmas before is pulled over his head but not his ears, and beyond him lays a painterly landscape of meadows with old chicken coop jumps and stone walls.

"It sure is pretty," my father says. "I never tire of it. Never do."

Dad talks then about the land; what will become of it and what has already become of some of our favorite haunts and vistas. It is truly beautiful here, twenty miles west of Boston, a land full of undeveloped pockets of farmland and centuries-old houses. My father and I continue to dig for stories we can share as we move toward Hanson's Farm on skinny, winding roads, the old motor rising and falling with the shifting of gears. We have bought vegetables from Chink Hanson since I was a small child and Chink and his boys have hayed our field for years.

We go right at the fork in the road, and Dad updates me on Penelope Turton, a terribly British old vegan; she died last year. She lived in a tiny house next to her farm just up on the left.

"She was weird (*wee-erd*)," my father says, his Boston accent pronounced. "Always hailing the virtues of organic vegetables. Blek."

I think about our history with organic gardening and laugh.

"They are small!" He's still arguing about it. "Too damn small."

We smoke happily, away now from the gaze of my mother, who, since quitting years before, has forbidden smoke in the house. Our plumes of smoke are invisible in the wind, but we can feel the heat in our chests as we throw our ashes to the air. My father and I have smoked together for years, Daddy-o always a handy bum, a Winston never far from his grasp. As a teenager and beyond, I often poked my fingers into the front pocket of his T or dress shirt to help myself, also patting his pocket for a light. Exasperated, he'd dig around to help me while complaining, *The next thing you know you'll be asking for a pat on the back to start you puffing.*

Everyone else in the family has quit. Even my sister, one of the big smokers, quit two or three years ago, but Pops and I continue even under the threat of cancer.

"What difference would it make now?" my father asks, to which I have no answer except silence. *Dad, this smoking business is killing us. We are a dying breed. Ha-ha-ha.* I look at my Dad's face and his ashen skin and think about the vegetables at Penelope Turton's large, hearty garden. *Organics? Blek.*

We make our way past the Quaker Meeting House, up old Nixon Road, and into the driveway of Hanson's Farm. This has become a tradition: Visit home; go to Hanson's with Dad to see how Chink has fared with the fruits and vegetables my father doesn't grow. We go into the old dairy barn and wend our way through the aisles. The displays are made of crates and old barrels; produce sits in boxes on the cement floor. The back of the building is wide open, and in the distance a green blanket of beans moves in the afternoon wind. My father pokes through the peaches.

"They look lousy," he says.

"Good for pies," I offer and throw a few in a bag. "Cobbler?" I suggest. My father sticks out his tongue at me and I put them back.

He has grown picky about these things: He knows a good peach when he sees one, knows the perfect crispness of green beans as sure as he knows his name.

"The strawberries last year were awful," he says, "but the beans . . ." He licks his lips. "Chink does a good job with the beans."

I know he feels like hell and is trying to be cheerful.

"Hello, Mr. Montgomery," the woman behind the cash register says. She is small with blond hair and has hints of peach lipstick at the center of her bottom lip.

"Hello there," my father says. "How's the corn?"

"Good, good."

"That's good. Last year's was horrible." My father lifts his shoulders in one smooth movement as if his body is surprised by his comment.

"Too wet," she says with a smile.

"Is that what it was?" He picks at an ear, pulls down the silk, and seeing a few rotten spots, puts it back.

"I guess we'll pass today."

He moves around to rest in front of the beans, where he grabs handfuls and pushes them into a paper bag.

I wander, pushing my fingers in the piles of vegetables in the bins, remembering a day of summer camp held here, drinking sour milk and throwing up or wetting my pants or both, and recall how all the Hanson boys near my age have the same round, serene face, the only difference being slightly different shades to their hair.

"C'mon kid," my father yells as he walks out, the paper bag of beans bouncing at his side. "You're holding me up."

As I run to get in the car, I see us as we were maybe thirty years ago, me running to keep up. People called me Tiny for being the youngest of the family and told me that I looked just like my father.

On the trip home he recounts again the time we fished together at the lake where we summered when I was very small. We woke long before sunrise and snuck out the porch door together.

"Do you remember that?" he asks.

I say yes, but in truth the memory is incomplete. It remains broken into fragments of sounds and pictures—the swinging and slam of a porch door and the smell of lake and gas melded together. The orange of the life jacket, always pulled too tight. The sound of the rope snapping from the outboard motor. The motor catching: The dark glassiness of a lake still in slumber. There the memory ends.

That night we eat dinner quietly. My mother is asleep, and I am nervous as I watch my father struggle to chew and swallow.

"Hmm," he says. "These beans are good."

Since his retirement, Daddy-o has become a stickler in the kitchen. He has grown picky about the amount of water used for steaming and the precise height of the oven rack for broiling. Tonight we cook filet of sole, and as we sit for a moment, I feel the way I often do here, biding time, a little lonely for my childhood, when our lives were firmly melded together. For years and years, things seemed the same, and then suddenly, in an instant, my father is an old man.

Dad chews strangely now. He sits almost on the edge of his chair, struggling to swallow, then shaking his head as if to say, *No, this will not work.* He slides quickly out of his chair, walks to the bathroom, and begins to heave. I look around for help but see only my reflection in the dark windows and, at my feet, Inky, the dog. She barks for a treat and I look over to the photographs on the bulletin board, the stacks of paper piled on car and business magazines on the counter, while I listen to my father choke and spit. I stand and walk to the doorway of the bathroom to find him bent over the sink pulling yards of white stringy mucous from deep in his throat; there is a pause and then, choking, he pulls more. He throws a glance into the mirror in between heaves and wipes away the tears, which seem to come not from sadness so much as exertion and shock—as if to say, *What in the hell is happening to me?*

5

THE DIAGNOSIS

October 1998
Boston, Massachusetts

There is nothing in the world like my father's face. I want to stop strangers and tell them everything about it. His perfectly shaped eyebrows, the dip in his upper lip. All the different ways it can look: Happy face. Fat face. Mad face. Patient face. A gentle face. The face of a wise man. A stupid man. A responsible, loyal man. My father is a man who wears glasses. His eyes are small and close together. Mother always told us we were built the same way, like ponies: short and sturdy.

"You look just like him," she says, "especially around the eyebrows."

I have my father's eyebrows and his legs, short and thick, sausagelike with monstrous knees.

Dad, I tell him, *our knees are so big we could hide things in them.*

Like what?

Small children. Bags of pot. An African village.
Ha!

My father's face is something I know deeply in my center. He has the half smile of a handsome man. His full smile, if ever present, is tentative. He has a heart-shaped birthmark on his throat, and on afternoons when I go through old photographs, I find it.

Actually there are very few photographs of my family together, but there is one, a Polaroid black-and-white taken in 1960 at the lake in New Hampshire, where we spent summers until 1965, and where mother and father had summered with their families. That's where they met, when they were both seventeen. In the photo, Mother is a babe at forty, a bottle blonde; she sits with her eyes closed. Beside her Dad smirks, dressed in his favorite checkered shirt. Lael, at twelve, has her finger in her eye. Bob is ten, a boy staring at his shoes. And on Mumzy's lap, me, three years old.

There are two dead babies, too. You can't see them in the photo, but we all know they are there. When I am a child and Mother feels sad on their birthdays I imagine them moving through me like weather, like little gusts of hot wind, warm spots in a lake. The first was a girl, born in 1945. The boy came two years later. They both died of brain hemorrhages when they were a few days old. No one knows the actual name of the condition, we are only told it is an incompatibility of the blood platelets. Strangely, the dead babies were named Lael and Bob. The surviving Lael and Bob, and I, are alive because we were transfused at birth.

After another unsuccessful biopsy attempt, Dad and I arm ourselves with medical records from the Framingham Hospital. We drive through Natick, Newton, and Wellesley, drifting toward Boston to meet with the fancy oncologists at the Dana-Farber Institute to talk about surgery. A few weeks before, my sister Lael, my brother Bob, and I spent days on the telephone to find the best surgeon, the best opinion, and the best oncologist for gastrointestinal disorders. We worked through different channels, from different coasts, but all arrived at the best in the city—a surgeon and oncologist whom my father, my brother, and I plan on meeting this morning.

My father drives along Route 9, an old stagecoach route that goes from Worcester to Boston. We drive through all the towns, passing old turnoffs to schools, riding lessons, and my mother's childhood home in Newton.

"Are you scared?" I ask him.

"No. Not scared. I don't know what to be scared about yet."

"Worried?"

"Yes, worried. I don't know what the hell is going on."

We talk about cars, always a popular topic with my father.

"They do a good job with the Buick," he says.

This is the car we drive, a blue Buick, a car my father adores and because he adores it, I do, too, every part of it, its shape, its color, the smell of cigarettes, and the light-blue leather of the interior.

It seems we drive this Buick on this highway millions of times, having the same conversations about Buick, about Ford and Ferrari, Ford and Saab and Jaguar.

My husband Tom has a love affair with the Saab, pronounced "sob," and deplores American car makers. My father pronounces Saab like "tab" and drives only American cars.

"Poor Tommy," my father says. "He'll be so sad about Ford buying Saab."

All in all, we make forty trips in and out of Boston, up and down the old Post Road, to and from the hospital, and throughout all these journeys, I watch us from the corner of my eye. I watch me watch him. Pop against autumn leaves. Pop against a summer white. Pop against the green of spring. We drive through time—during our trips back and forth between home and the cancer center, and later, chemotherapy and the ER, I revisit all the drives of our life together: to and from schools, riding lessons, horse shows, the drug store, the supermarket, the grain store, the hardware store. And on each drive now, I watch my father look out the window, and wonder if he ever thinks about seeing this landscape for the last time. I turn and watch it all blur by, all the walls and stone houses, reservoirs, and more stone houses on dams, antique and photo stores and shopping malls, through all the places of our lives. I imagine my father as a young man, courting my mother, driving this same route from Worcester, where he went to school at Worcester Polytech, to my mother's house, and then later, their drives together to Boston for the births of us.

These are the times I begin to know my father, when he begins to die. Going to and from the hospital, my father tells me about his life. Finally, I am old enough to see him as a man, and not just as my father.

This is the only time my father talks about the dead babies.

"Your mother was never the same," my father says. "Nope. She wasn't ever the same."

For the first baby, Dad was in the Pacific, an ensign in the Navy during World War II. "The letters were mixed up," he said, "so I didn't know what to make of it. I received a letter telling me about giving away all the baby's clothes. I hadn't received the letter about the baby girl dying in your mother's arms five days after she was born."

Other details of their deaths have leaked out over the years. They disposed of them in hospital incinerators, so there were no funerals, no ceremonies to mark their short lives.

For the second baby, two years later, a boy, my father was home from the war. "A few days after he was born, we stayed up all night looking for a doctor in the hospital," he said. "Your mother was convinced there was something wrong, but no one would listen. The boy died the next morning."

In my mind, I watch him tell this story over and over. His face moves into confusion; a blank bewilderment. *I spent all night walking up and down the halls looking for a doctor to help us, and not one would. Can you imagine?*

Watching out of the windows of the car as he talks, I construct pictures of my parents as a young couple. I see my father walk in circles around a now defunct maternity hospital called the Boston Lying-In, and in a small room nearby, my mother's twenty-four-year-old face as she receives the news that her second baby has died.

In the beginning of my father's illness, we know very little. There's talk about esophageal cancer, and it's on this drive to discuss surgery with the doctors that I learn more because we finally have the records:

The mass appears to involve much of the stomach. The abnor-
mality measures 6 x 10 centimeters . . . near the fundus and body
with apparent extension to involve the cardio-esophageal junction
and inferior extension to at least abut the body and tail of pancreas.
Question is raised regarding some involvement of the adjacent
splenic artery along the medial aspect of the mass. Obstructive lung
disease.

"Did you read this?" I hold up the record and shake it.

"Yep."

"What do you think?"

"I don't know what to think, Lee, I really don't."

"What's with the obstructive lung disease?"

"Got me," he says.

He looks at me. I look at him.

And we drive.

I sink further down into the seat and turn to him.

The tracks of the comb are still present in his hair, and his nose is large and shaped oddly, like a piece of dough.

"It keeps growing," he told me once. "That and the ears." He reached a hand up and pulled a lobe.

We pass the white monstrosity of the Chestnut Hill Mall and I feel the end of my nose with a finger, remembering how, when I was little, my father could steal it, capturing it between two fingers. He feigned struggling a bit at first, trying to pry it off—and then with great flourish pulled in one quick motion. "Got it," he said and then spun around and quickly hid his hands behind his back. I was mystified. *My nose?* He laughed and presented a thumb wedged between his two fingers that looked remarkably like my nose. Years later, when we drive I feel his fingers clasp my nose with such authority and skill it is nothing short of magic.

∞

Dana-Farber is a shiny, well-endowed cancer institute that prides itself on providing "the finest adult cancer care available anywhere in the world." We walk the halls and ride the elevators with bald people and are silent as we face bulletin boards holding fliers with names like the Jimmy Fund and American Cancer Society, newsletters about prostate and breast cancer support groups. We look at each other, eyes wide, lips buttoned, in awe of the new world we are entering.

Bob meets us in the waiting room, and when he walks in, I realize I can't remember the last time I saw him. It was most likely the year before, but it seems like a decade. He's wearing glasses now, and his hair is gray. We are here early, maybe two hours before the appointment, because of the genetic predisposition of all Montgomery males to be early. Lael and I have joked for a long time about how Dad has to be at the airport two days before his plane departs because he missed that one plane in 1974 on his way to San Francisco.

A computer sits in the middle of the waiting room among peach carpets, overstuffed couches, and pretty patterned upholstered chairs. I use it to pull up information on esophageal and stomach cancers. When I turn to Bob and Dad behind me to share hopeful things, they are both reading magazines, their ankles crossed in the same way, licking fingers to turn pages.

Then my father's name is called, and we herd ourselves into a small room to meet The Surgeon. He wears a gray suit and has his hair cut like a British schoolboy's, all of which tells us he went to Harvard or Dartmouth or Yale, which impresses us because we didn't. He has very small teeth, which he barely shows. His accent is affected Boston Brahmin and his eyes are so small I can barely see the whites or irises. After a few moments and a brief examination, he delivers the absolute worst news, of which I hear only fragments (*Tumor . . . stomach . . . large . . . twisted . . . aorta . . . Concern . . . lung . . . survive. . . Nasty . . . untreatable . . . Won't know . . . Opened . . .*) because I'm obsessed with watching my brother wiggle in his chair and jitter his feet. I turn to my father, who is smiling, shrugging his shoulders, and having trouble breathing, but not admitting it.

"Well, what you say sounds pretty bleak," my father says.

I turn to The Surgeon, thinking he couldn't possibly mean what he is saying.

"Yes, well, it is," he says, not offering anything else, not one strand of hope anywhere, and no movement indicating discomfort.

My father sits looking at The Surgeon, smiling, his shoulders slipping around his ears. In his hand is a list of questions written entirely in capital letters.

DIAGNOSIS
1. HOW SURE
2. AGREE WITH D.F. METROWEST
3. WHEN WILL WE KNOW FOR SURE

TREATMENT
1. SURGERY
   A. WHEN-WHERE
   B. BLOOD. FAMILY

C. TIME IN HOSPITAL
D. RECUPERATION PERIOD
   1. HOW LONG
   2. FEEDING
   3. AT HOME
   4. WHAT HELP IS AVAILABLE

All of which he can't ask. I watch as his eyes move over the piece of paper and see he has written in the corner: *Big Operation. Lung Damage. Increases risk. Epidural. Keep out for a few days.*

He also holds another piece of paper with directions to the cancer center, and, later in the day, he receives another piece of notepaper with a drug name, Fareston (toremifene citrate) printed on the bottom in fuchsia and orange letters, and The Surgeon's cartoon drawing of a stomach being cut at top and bottom. *Most likely stomach,* the doctor wrote while in our meeting. *Palliative surgery for dysphasia.*

I don't remember much of this because I am looking at my father smiling and shrugging his shoulders, now a small, old man as he receives this news. I would have thought that the world crashing down around a man would make a sound, but there is nothing. My father smiles as if the surgeon were talking about a carburetor. I watch him and wonder how is it possible that such information can come at him and move so quickly inside to become invisible. Suddenly, I cannot breathe.

I ask questions but they don't come out in any sensible order; all of my words are garbled and my voice shakes and I feel ashamed that my words are stuck in the back of my throat. Everything I ask The Surgeon is met with No. No. No.

"What about chemotherapy options, clinical trials?" I ask.

"The newer clinical trials," he says, "are usually reserved for younger people."

I look at his hands folded together on his lap and see they are small and delicate and shiny. They look like hands that play the piano at night after days spent slipping inside people, pulling, tearing at arteries, pushing at organs.

"Excuse me," I mutter as I get up. I am afraid I am about to fall apart, so I leave the room.

When I return, another man introduces himself as The Oncologist. He looks to be about twenty, handsome-handsome-handsome with pointy shoes and a compassionate tilt to his head. A smile. He leans against the examining table with his hands grasping the tabletop behind him, his head tilted just so. I am encouraged because I believe he is not only caring but also hopeful. He basically tells us the same thing that The Surgeon did up to a point. Then he contradicts him. He says until the biopsy gives a diagnosis, it's impossible to begin a chemotherapy regime. "The tumor needs to be removed," he says quietly. "If we cannot remove it, Dr. X will put in a feeding tube and we can consider chemotherapy protocols. If Dr. X can remove the tumor . . ."

My mind hits the brakes at feeding tube and I think, *my father will be nourished as he dies,* but The Oncologist keeps talking as if there is hope and I cannot stop looking at his lips. I ask him about clinical trials and unlike The Surgeon, he says, *Oh, yes, this is a possibility,* and I begin to feel warm and otherwordly, as if anything is possible, as if our lives were part of some television show like *Touched by an Angel* or *ER* where people not only save lives, but find true love, too.

Later when Dad and I climb into the car and drive west toward home, he talks nonstop. He talks as if he will never be able to talk again. He talks about his mother, his father, his brothers, about getting his affairs in order in case he does not live. As he talks, I ask questions. I nod. I drive. I cry. I nod some more. I keep driving. What is he talking about? He's talking about sad things, and I hardly remember any of them. He is talking about his life as a man, not as my father, and all I can do is cry and think about a game my husband and I play when I feel sad.

Do you want to be touched by an angel? he asks. And when I nod, he places a pretend wand on my head and softly says, *Ding! Ding! Ding!*

Ahead, taillights smear jagged red lines down the highway. My father looks out the window, still talking, talking, talking, about what I don't know. All I can think about are lost things—years, his father's first car, a Packard with a broken axle sinking in a cornfield, and all those stories he told me about milking cows and hating it.

The Surgeon's notes from this meeting are as follows:

Robert Montgomery is a 76-year-old male who has a four-month history of difficulty swallowing and weight loss. During that time he has lost approximately 24 pounds, down to approximately 139 pounds. He has not had any overt bleeding. He has no evidence of congestive heart failure. He smokes a pack of cigarettes a day, and is slightly short of breath in conversation. However, he claims that he can walk up two flights of stairs without being short of breath. The upper GI series was reviewed and a narrowing of the esophogastric junction was noted. The narrowing continues for approximately 10 cm in the stomach. CAT scan shows a mass lesion at that level. A lymph node appears to be enlarged adjacent to the celiac access. Despite the lack of a tissue diagnosis, I think the overwhelming evidence is in favor of gastric carcinoma.

6

SURGERY

November 1998
Boston, Massachusetts

Sometimes, when I think of my family, I imagine a miniature solar system. We are the earth, the sun, and the moon,
and outer planets. Father is the deeply rooted earth. Mother
is a hot and fiery sun, big enough to fill up the sky. Lael is
Saturn with all her pretty-colored rings, and Bob is Jupiter,
a sad boy with many moons, and big ears like Dumbo.

"Why not Pluto?" Lael asks. "Bobby is far away; he
should be Pluto."

"His head's too fat."

"You're right. He does have a fat head," she laughs. "Fathead. Fathead. God, how he hated it when I called him
that."

The dead Lael and Bob are like invisible stars. And I am
the moon, moving around everyone and everything, moving around my sister and brother, around father, who moves
around Mother, who just moves around, all of us rising and

sinking behind invisible horizons. I have spent a lifetime haunted by us.

There might be a name for this condition: Loveusmotherfatherus? Loveusallofus? Loveusdreamofus.

It could be a bona fide chemical imbalance like Lael says. When she is in graduate school at Harvard, she calls me to read my diagnosis from the *Diagnostic and Statistical Manual of Mental Disorders* (the DSM).

"This sounds like you," she says and then reads out the most horrifying sounding conditions like this: *dissociative identity disorder, borderline personality, manic-depressive, bipolar disease.*

Okay, I think, Okay, I might have eaten too much acid in high school.

And?

Okay, I did. I smoked a lot of pot and ate a phenomenal amount of LSD in high school. White Lightning, Orange Sunshine. Microdot. Windowpane. And then, of course, we were all supposed to be retarded.

"Did you know anything about that?" I ask. "Because of the transfusions? Mother said we were supposed to be retarded."

Lael is silent.

Well? Did you?

Going back generations, our family has always been fond of complex and unpopular ideas, squandered lumber and copper fortunes, Tories, ship captains lost at sea, slave runners, and drunks of both the world class and garden variety. And cruelty, one can't forget that. Cruelty of the most peculiar kind; the kind generated by fear.

We are the *negativos.* We are an all-American family. *How do you do?*

∞

On the morning my father is scheduled to have surgery. Mother hands me a photograph.

"It's a good one," she says. "He's not an easy subject."

My father does not smile in photographs. Sometimes he even closes his eyes. In the photograph Mother hands me now, he is smiling wide. It is summer and behind him are the long turquoise rectangle of the pool and the lattice door of the pool house. He wears the watch that I now wear on my own wrist for safekeeping. The fingers of his left hand are cut off in the photograph; his right hand is clenched into a fist to hide the fingers he chopped up with the snow blower.

In this photograph my father's face is wrinkled by a moment when happiness invaded; his eyes squint so they appear partially closed. The photograph must have been taken around a meal because there appears to be the tiniest piece of Pepperidge Farm Toasting White between his teeth.

∞

The afternoon Dad is admitted to the hospital for surgery, Bob, Lael, and I spend hours with him in the waiting room. We wait for an EKG. We wait for blood work. We talk to a young woman who—despite advanced ovarian cancer—is full of life and stories about getting married. She makes us all laugh. A lot. "She is a live wire," my father says, shaking his head and laughing. "She is a real pissa."

At the end of the day, we find our father's hospital room at the end of a hall. Outside the windows, two towers loom in the distance, looking nuclear. Dad lies down on the hospital bed and closes his eyes. The three of us flit about, getting water, bossing nurses, worrying about the view, until he finally tells us to go home. He will be taken down for his surgery the following morning at six, and we plan to meet then to see him off. "Wow, that's early," he says. "I wouldn't bother if I were you."

I sit on the edge of his bed and take his hand. He purses his lips as if trying to smile despite his exhaustion. "There's no place we'd rather be than here with you."

"Okay," he says, embarrassed by our attention, "but God it's early."

He turns to stare out the darkened window, and then closes his eyes. I watch him for a while. There are so many things I want to say, but I remain silent. "I love you, Dad," I finally say, getting up to leave.

"I love you, too, Lee."

We are better at saying these things now than we used to be. Only a few years earlier, I had realized that, though I assumed my father loved me, he had never said so. For one spring, I was obsessed with getting him to say the words. At the end of every conversation, I would say, "I love you, Dad." And each time, I could hear him struggle with the return. "Yeah, yeah, yeah," he'd say, or "Me, too." Finally one day he said, without even thinking, "I love you too, kid."

The next morning, I awake at some ungodly hour and wander the house in darkness, moving down the stairs to turn on the coffee. I walk through the living room to find Stoyan sound asleep on the couch. He had arrived in the middle of the night after playing his clarinet into the wee hours in some bar in Cambridge. I walk into my parents' room and find my mother in darkness. "Hey," she says. Mother's voice has never changed, and though she would be considered an elderly woman at the age of seventy-eight, her voice remains young and strong.

"Hi," I say.

"Did Stoyan get in okay?" she asks.

"Yeah, he's asleep on the couch."

I sit for a second on the edge of the bed, half asleep, smelling my mom, a weird combination of gin and sandwich meat, lipstick and perfume. It is a smell I know well from afternoons in my childhood when she passed out from too much gin. I was lonely, and wanted her to wake up, so I'd crawl around on her and pull her tongue and stick my fingers in her nose, while I waited, waited, and waited for my father to come home. She never did wake up, even when my small fingers were able to block her breath. When I held her nose, she opened her mouth. When I blocked her mouth, she breathed through her nose.

When Pop finally would arrive, he would look at Mother sadly. "Well, it appears as if your mother didn't have her nap." During those evenings, we worked around her, but when I was in high school, the nap became our Morse code. "Has your mother had her nap?" which meant, of course, is your Mother bombed? Have you had your dinner?

"Are you getting up?" I ask.

"Good God, yes," she says.

"What time is it?" I hear Lael ask. Even in the darkness

I can see her silhouette in the doorway, dressed in her flannel nightshirt, her arms folded in front of her. She gets into bed with Mother, pulling the covers around her.

"Brrr," she says.

"I don't know. Four?"

We have to get Mother up and fix her breakfast, the logistics of pulling out cereal boxes and half-gallon cartons of milk too much for her, with her buggy and only one good arm. As Lael waits on Mom, I busy myself with setting up an altar on the kitchen table. It's made of a Lady Guadalupe candle, branches, and flowers from my father's garden. I place the flowers and branches on the silver platter around a silver hunting trophy bowl that I fill with water. I place the candle in the bowl so it will remain cool. When I step back, it looks holy.

"Make sure the candle stays lit," I tell Mother as we head toward the door.

"Okay," she says.

She looks so sad sitting there, I return and kiss her.

"We'll call you all day, all the time."

She nods, looking like a lost child, and I turn to leave.

"Wait a minute," she says, taking off her high school ring to pull off a gold band.

"I've been married to myself. He won't wear it." She hands it to me.

"What do you want me to do, Mum?"

"When he comes out of surgery, put it on him, but make sure he's asleep."

I look at it, splayed out in the palm of my hand, a simple gold band, my father's wedding ring, a ring he can no longer wear because it is too small.

∽∾

As the sky grows pink with the dawn's light, Lael, Bob, and I sit with Daddy-o as he gets high on his first installment of knockout drugs. Dad is wearing a queer blue surgical hat made of netting.

"Are you stoned?" I ask Dad.

"I don't think so," he says, pursing his lips, moving his toes.

"Hey, Dad," my brother says. "How many fingers?"

"Beats the hell out of me," Dad says, smiling.

Bobby smiles, looks at me from over the tops of his glasses.

"Big Dad is stoned," he says. "Nice hat, Dad." as he pats his head, feeling his new hat.

A moment later, we follow the orderly as he guides our father's gurney through the halls to the elevators to the waiting room next to the operating room. I hold onto my father's feet as we go, terrified that this is the end of him. I watch Bob and Lael's faces: when they are not making jokes and moving smiles across their lips, they look at their shoes.

Thankfully, the anesthesiologist is a card. He knows people we know, namely a psychologist whom Lael and I saw during the roaring eighties until she lost her license for dealing cocaine. This makes Lael and me laugh. Remember *that?* The anesthesiologist has red hair, and freckles on his knuckles. I ask him to request that The Surgeon (we've been calling him Sourpuss) tell a joke or two to reassure my father before they put him under. The anesthesiologist, busy plunging narcotics into my father's veins to relax him before he is wheeled into the operating room, looks up and smiles a little.

"You mean Smiling Bob?" he asks.

"Is that what you call him?"

He nods.

This makes us all laugh and when they wheel our Pops, stretched on the gurney, through those doors, *whoppawhoppa,* he is laughing and waving bye-bye. My brother yells something again about how much he loves Dad's new hat.

When the doors close and our father is gone, our eyes again drop to our shoes, the white tiles of the linoleum floor. We are deep in the basement of the Brigham Hospital, several floors below street level, with hours to go.

∞

While seventy-seven-year-old John Glenn makes last-minute preparations to orbit the world, a team of surgeons remove a tumor from my father's stomach, a tumor the size and thickness of two Webster's Collegiate dictionaries, ninth edition, with tentacles that crept through organs and his pericardium toward his heart, eating into his spleen and pancreas. With many hands they remove it all, snipping and removing pieces of his organs as they go, the spleen, the tail of the pancreas, the lower third of the esophagus, two-thirds of his stomach, tying off arteries and veins, buttoning things back up. *Heave-ho, one-two-three,* it spills into a stainless steel pan, its web torn, leaving its invisible ends in lymph nodes, on kidney, liver, and bone.

∽

Late that afternoon, our father has two questions.

"Is it cancer?" is the first.

He turns toward me: His head moves chaotically, his eyes roll as he struggles to open them. I can barely hear him because his mouth is under an oxygen mask, the rest of him full of plugs and wires and pumps.

"Did it spread?" is the second.

Then he slips back into unconsciousness. Bobby, Lael, and I stand by his bed. When he opened his eyes a few minutes earlier we all screamed, pushing ourselves into view, waving hello. We were exhausted with waiting; licking our fingers, Lael and I moving through empty magazines, Bobby reading the same page of a novel in Italian, all of us holding our breath in the family waiting room as five hours moved like glaciers. When the call finally came from The Surgeon, each of us sat motionless with our own picture of Dad being wheeled away in his new blue hat. Lael and I pushed Bob to answer the phone. He turned away from us and pushed a finger into his ear so he could hear. A minute later, he pointed a triumphant thumb into the air. Lael and I crowded around him, but when he hung up, he was silent, only waving a hand. He led us into a family room, shut the door, and sat down, but didn't say a word. Instead, he removed his glasses and began to cry, burying his head in a palm, periodically pushing one thumb in the air. Lael and I knew nothing except that Pops was alive. We cried, too, and the three of us fell one by one into disorderly heaps of relief on the desks and in chairs.

For the hours following the surgery, we are allowed to visit intensive care every hour for five minutes.

"Don't touch him," my brother says during one visit. When I see my father's eyes struggle to open, I place my hands on his forehead. Each time I do, my father pushes his consciousness to the surface. Bob wants him to rest. I want to reassure our father.

My father struggles to pull off his oxygen mask to tell us this: "I am a very sick boy."

Lael stands still. She is our leader—the eldest, the boldest, the brightest—now subdued by a cold and terror that is apparent even behind the large tortoiseshell glasses that make her look like Atom Ant.

Days later, the doctors do not tell my father the truth about his cancer—and neither do I.

"What did they say?" I ask.

"Oh, it's just an ordinary cancer," Dad says.

"They didn't say anything else?"

"Nope."

I have spent days on the Internet so I know that ordinary gastric cancer has a 10 percent survival rate at best.

From the hospital, I call my brother at work and don't mention this news. Instead, I harass him.

"Hey, Bob," I say. "Guess what?"

"What?"

"I'm touching him, Bob. I'm touching Dad all over."

Bob laughs.

"Oh, Bobbolou," I say in singsong. "I'm touching him all over. You better get here quick."

Later, my father is moved from the bed near the window to the bed closest to the door.

"Is there any mail," he asks.

He's got a weird expression on his face.

"Were you out at the mailbox? Was there any mail?"

"No, Dad. You're in the hospital."

He doesn't say anything else, and I know something is terribly wrong.

I run into the hallway and yell for a nurse, and when no one responds, I race around the floor yelling, searching for someone to help. When a nurse finally comes in, she sees Dad's blood pressure diving to dangerous levels. She runs out of the room and back in very quickly and then plunges a syringe into his IV, watching as the numbers on the digital monitor come back up.

"There," she says.

I watch his blood pressure on the monitor obsessively for an hour, but then we sleep. I am in a chair, while my father stretches out in his hospital bed like a king. As evening comes, and I open my eyes, I catch him in a private moment as he explores the apparatus moving in and out of his body. His fingers touch the tubes in his nose, arm, and chest and then follow them from his body to each machine, tugging a little to find each source and destination. He taps a pump, the IV machine, what he might call the lung-sucker-outer. His lips purse in concentration, his eyes curious and concerned.

On Halloween, five days after surgery, my father laughs all day. He is wearing the red devil horns I brought him, and flirting with the nurses who move in and out of the room. "Boo," he says.

As each day passes, the nurses remove another tube—the ones my father hasn't removed himself. Two days after his surgery, he phones home at seven in the morning. We are so delighted that he remembers how to dial a phone that we run to pick up different phones in the house. His voice sounds stronger, more like him.

"The nurses are all mad at me."

"Why?"

"I removed my tube."

"Jesy Christmas, Monty," Mother says.

"What tube?" I ask.

"How the hell would I know."

"Dad, where did you take it out of?" Lael asks.

"I think my nose."

"You took the tube out of your nose?" my mother says.

"I guess so," Dad says.

"Was it hard to get out?" I ask.

"No, not at all," Dad says.

I imagine my father, fascinated by all the machinery, poking and pulling at tubes, pushing buttons on the machines to see what they're made of. I imagine him arriving at this tube taped in his nose, slowly peeling off the tape and beginning to tug, slowly, painstakingly, finger by finger, feeling perhaps a strange sensation in his chest, since this tube moves from his nose into what's left of his stomach. Perhaps he chokes a little as the head of the tube comes through his throat, but he doesn't say.

"Did it hurt?" I ask.

"Don't think so."

That afternoon, during another sleepy visit, the nurses change the dressings around his chest and stomach and I see the scar that moves from his armpit, across his chest, and down his torso like a twisted Z from Zorro.

"Frankenpops," I say.

"Nah," he says, looking out the window onto the wall of another hospital building.

"Frankendaddy-o?" I suggest.

He smiles.

"Better," he says, not moving his eyes.

We fall asleep again until another doctor arrives. She is sweet, young enough to pass as a teenager, cute enough that my father flirts mercilessly. After looking him over, she tells him she'll be back later.

"What time would that be?" he asks.

"What time?" she repeats.

"That's what I said. What time can I expect you?"

"Are you going somewhere?" she asks.

"Well, I have a golf game scheduled for three," and then we begin to giggle loudly. We both know he doesn't play the game.

∽

A few days later, I call The Surgeon's office to get the pathology report.

"Hi Peggy, did the pathology come back?"

"Let's see," she says. "I think it's two out of three. Yep. Perogastric, perisplenic . . ."

"What does it mean?"

"Well, let's put it this way. It will get him in the end."

"Did you tell him that?"

"No," she says. "We want to give them hope so they recover."

I put down the phone and look at Mother.

"Well?" she says.

"It looks great," I lie. "He's going to be fine."

7

MIRACLES

Summer 1997
Framingham, Massachusetts

On a hot summer day a few years before my father gets sick Mother's head flips around like she's a rag doll. She is singing a song for me. Stoyan is new here, but Mom is already calling him Sweet Stuff. He accompanies her on the piano, which he plays ploddingly, one note at a time.

She makes a recording as she sings, so we can spend the rest of the day listening while making sad faces at one another. I don't know this song, but I cry because it is heartbreaking and true.

"Hello there, good old friend of mine,
You've been reaching for yourself for such a long, long time."

I hadn't visited Framingham for a few years, and now, sitting five feet away from her in the same room, it still feels like there's a continent between us.

A few days later, I return to my home with Tom in Los Angeles and soon afterwards, I drive up the Ventura Freeway to see Lael and Jon, in from San Diego visiting friends in Westlake Village. I bring the tape of Mother singing and a tape recorder. Lael and I sit down together and I plug it in. The sadness is palpable in Mother's voice, a sadness that hangs in our own faces, along with something else, but it is too much to think or talk about. I say to Lael, "Can you believe this? Can you believe this?"

Mother's voice is low and she drunkenly half sings and half talks, a cross between Sarah Vaughan and Bob Dylan.

"Oh, brother," Lael says.

Lael and I didn't become friends until I graduated from college, and not good friends until I was in my thirties when we both lived in California. Before this time, our history as sisters living together in Framingham sits mostly empty, a white space. I was only three when she began attending a private day school in Wellesley, and ten when she left, never to live with us again.

Lael has memories of me when I was very young, and over the years she prodded me.

Do you remember your velour brown hat? That stupid hat? You wore it everywhere.

No.

Do you remember when we dressed you up in Mother's wedding dress and put you in a cage on the wagon and dragged you through the neighborhood?

No.

When we sent you through the back of the convertible to the trunk so you could hand us all our Christmas presents?

No.

Do you remember getting drunk when you were three?

No.

Do you remember that great French bathing suit I brought you from Paris?

Yes.

I had a better chance of knowing Bob. We had a few more years living together and after he left for college he still came home for the summers. When I was twelve or thirteen, and Bob and Susan were living in Providence, students at the Rhode Island School of Design, they would drop by and Susan would brush my hair. It was very long and I had the worst time brushing out all the snarls. She never spoke when she did it, but would spend quiet, painstaking hours gently separating the gargantuan rat's nest on my head.

After I got my driver's license, I spent many weekends with them in a tiny Massachusetts coastal town on Buzzards Bay, playing cards with Susan, hammering out chords—C, D, G, A, E again and again—on Bob's guitar. Bob played the fiddle, and he and his friends would play bluegrass together. I spent days listening to them play and falling in and out of love with my brother's friends.

All throughout my childhood, I was allowed into Bob's world for brief visits, but I was enough his junior that he didn't encourage me to hang out for too long. Big Bob always seemed incredibly cool, and for years I devotedly kept track of what he was up to. When he was ten, he and his friends built a tree house in a big elm at the bottom of the field. A few years later, they stole my sister's friends' bras, tacked them up inside the tree house, and started a club called Bras Anonymous. I was never formally invited, and it wasn't until long after it was abandoned that I found my way up the ladder to see for myself. The ladder was covered in moss and missing many rungs, and the tree house was empty and barely intact, but I filled in all the blanks, imagining what was once there.

The same is true for the guts and eyeball club Lael and Bob set up in the attic of the barn. I have little memory of the actual event. God knows if I was even alive, but I have many memories of walking up and down the stairs in the barn to read the faded remains of the long, evil discourses they had written on the walls with window putty.

And this is the story. As a child, I was alone most of the time, surrounded by animals and beautiful countryside, inhabiting the places and stories where my brother and sister had once been, and where I imagined their lives and mine. It was in these empty spaces that I created my first fiction: my family, idealized, a perfect father, mother, sister, and brother.

I was very small when I learned to live in a made-up world. I studied my picture books intently, there were endless portraits of happy girls in petticoats. At five, I became a connoisseur of petticoats, collecting as many as I could, wearing them all at the same time.

Of course, people can't actually *live* in pretend worlds for very long. They can't die in them, either.

∞

One late afternoon in early November following Dad's surgery, I walk under a New England sky so beautiful it makes me weep. I watch the sun sweep color across the sky. To the east, the early winter horizon is a desperate white. To the west, the colors move from soft blues and pinks to deep charcoal toward night. I stand in the middle of it, in a corn field, and wish for impossible things: Time travel. Clocks turning back. Organs returned. The ocean meeting the back of our field.

The area remains rural. The houses are hundreds of years old and still surrounded by hay fields, meadows, and stone walls. I follow the long grassy carriage ways that lead around ponds, over wooden bridges, past a grist mill, and into the woods, where the trails are carpeted in places with pine needles, in other places with brightly dying leaves. There is the musty smell of dirt and water and autumn, and in memory, the peculiar sharpness of pony and cigarettes.

My father is now missing most of his stomach. He has no spleen. He is missing the tail of his pancreas. How does it happen that a man can live without these essential parts? When I look at him, I imagine that empty space in the middle and hear imaginary sounds—snorts and soft clatter, the slapping echoes of wet organs knocking around. I want to put it all back. Like a child armed with magical finger and paint, I want to return my father's organs to their rightful home. He has a quarter of a stomach, the size of a small pocket, stitched to two tubes: esophagus and intestine. I try to imagine the package—stomach, spleen, tumor, et al.—at the bottom of the surgeon's bucket, the color of teeth or bone; yellow, slippery, monstrous. *Then what?* They chop it up and look at the pieces. Later, they take the pieces wrapped in paraffin and store them in the basement of the Brigham Hospital, along with pieces of other people. One day all of these parts will leave the hospital and travel to a special sanctuary where they are stored indefinitely. Eventually this is all that will be left of BD—sections of tumor and organ under glass.

When I return, I approach the house through the back field, where I find myself searching the tiniest of valleys, hunting for uneven earth to indicate where my favorite animals are buried. Under a number of smallish lumps lay a schnauzer squashed by a car (1986), my mother's pet mink, Jezebel (1975), Maryanne Bitch Cat (1970), another cat named Sara Suckface (1969), a fox hound named Bally Hoo (1969), a Great Dane or four, a squirrel named Sylvester, a raccoon, and a skunk named Tabu (1963.) There is a big lump where Happy Birthday, my pony who died in 1976, was buried.

Even though Mother always kept horses and strange animals, like many little girls, I dreamt of having my very own pony, and devoted some time to praying for one: *Dear God, Please send me a pony. Please send me a pony. Please. Please. Please.* One afternoon, when I was nine, a pony arrived. Mother and I stood in the driveway and cried while we watched a scrawny polka-dot creature back itself out of the horse trailer. Mother insisted he was a birthday present, though I knew that wasn't exactly true: My birthday was still four months away. But we could pretend; this pony *could* be a birthday present. His name was even Happy Birthday, and he was a very pretty little pony. When he grew healthy, big fat silver dapples decorated his body, and he had a white mane and tail. Still, I was not at all sure he counted as a real birthday present because the pony, sick with heaves, was cast off from a more fortunate girl whose father was the master of the Nashoba Valley Hunt Club. But I went along with it because it sounded pretty spectacular. "I got a pony for my seventh birthday," I lied. "Aren't I a lucky girl?"

His color changed from chestnut to gray according to season. His enormous dark pony eyes ate light like the black water of deep ponds. During winter afternoons when it was too cold and snowy to go out, he stood in his stall. I have imagined him watching each of us wind down the wooden ramp into the cellar of the barn at different times. There was my mother, her ice tinkling in her drink. And then I'd come to feed him, early in the evening. Sometimes, after I fed him, I'd grab his blanket and climb on top of him and, straddling him backwards, lay my head on his rump and sleep. And I waited until I heard the *ph-lump* of the car coming into the barn above me, the tires slapping across the wide wooden planks, the slam of the car door, a cough, the clomping of wing-tipped shoes, and the smell of cigarette smoke. It was time to go up; Pops was home.

8

RECOVERY

November 1998
Framingham, Massachusetts

My father lives, but we, his family, lose momentum: Time moves forward and backward all at once. I imagine that he lives, then that he dies. He lives. He dies. Around and around.

We circle him, hovering. *Did you do this?* we ask. *Or that? How about this? Have you tried . . . ?*

We buy books, consult doctors, scour the Internet, take notes.

We make notebooks in three-ring binders and Mead Composition books, documenting everything, believing this will make a difference. When I see Bob's notebook, I abandon mine and cede the responsibility to him and instead organize a food journal in a Day Runner, demanding that my father write down everything he eats, the results of all meetings, the telephone numbers of everyone. When he refuses, I do it for him and then convince my mother to delegate the responsibility to Stoyan. In the front of the book,

I write *Think Health!* in bold blue letters. I also write an affirmation on a fuchsia Post-it note that I stick to the inside front cover: *With each day, I feel better and stronger than ever.* I sign it with a tiny smiley face.

∞

In a late afternoon light, my father lies back in his easy chair and stares into space. I imagine he is thinking about dying, the long path to nowhere. After a moment, his hazel eyes focus and he sighs.

"I'm wondering what sounds good for dinner," he says.

I am relieved. He is a man without a stomach, and he is wondering what to eat. He looks at me, and smiles, and I see my grandmother so clearly in his face. If I try, I can almost conjure her old lady crackly voice telling and retelling her stories of homemade root beer, cotton battens in the crème puffs, the wonders of castor oil. She loved to talk about Dad's birth and how the doctor made her walk through a field of snow in the middle of the night to expedite her sluggish labor. She also loved to recount the day the doctor removed Dad's appendix on the dining room table. To her these were perfect examples of the logic and simplicity of her day, and clearly demonstrated (again) the benefits of being an old-fashioned New England girl. One of her favorite sayings was: *You modern girls puzzle me.*

My father called her "Mother." She called him Robert. Never Monty. Or Bob. *Robert,* said quickly, as if it had only one syllable. When the anesthesiologist asked my father's name, Pop said, "People like to call me Bob." Mother calls him Monty. Daddy. Your father. That Bastard. When Dad returns home without his stomach, I call him Popalicious. Papalouie. Daddy-o. Old man. The fossil. And we walk.

"I'm going for a walk," he announces frequently. He groans as he shifts the chair's footrest through its gears to the floor. At the bottom, he lifts his legs up and down in one smooth motion and stands.

"I'm coming." I run and gather a coat.

Twice a day we wander up and down the street, poking our heads into old barns, collecting leaves and orange berries.

"Oh, look at these," I say.

I walk off the road to break off a stick of the berries and hold it up for Dad.

"Sweet bitter," he says and stops, his hands bundled into his pockets. What he means is bittersweet, but he has somehow inverted the words.

"We used to collect those for Mother down by a stream near our house. On holidays, she would send us down."

I continue picking and he watches; clouds of his breath appear and dissipate in the cold air.

"There's other stuff too," he says. "I can't for the life of me remember what it's called."

Humph! He shakes his head, cocks an ear as if listening to its sounds.

"Nope. No longer there!"

We walk slowly along the roads. On each outing, we walk in a different direction, one of four. Our house sits where two roads intersect on the diagonal. The intersection is the basis for our home's name, Four Corner Farm.

"Ha!" My father *humphed* over the years. "Back acres would be more appropriate! Belly achers! A few lousy acres!"

We walk past other homes; many of our old neighbors have moved away. The furniture man next door whose wife hung herself in the hallway or closet—we were never sure—left a few years ago and the house was bought by a young couple who dug up the front yard and planted wildflowers.

"I don't have the heart to tell her that it looks like shit," my father says one morning when we walk by. He half smiles as if uncomfortable with his criticism.

"But it does. It looks like shit. I like lawns."

He wears a London Fog trench coat and keeps his hands in his pockets.

"Ha! Do you remember, Dad," I ask. "Do you remember Jennifer Bowen running into the house and yelling, 'Monty, your garage doors look like shit!'"

"Ha!" Dad says stopping, swaying a little on his feet like his mother once did, though her legs bowed as if she'd ridden horses every day for one hundred years.

For our afternoon walks we often walk up and down Winch Street, snipping more "sweet bitter" that I arrange in vases all through the house. The road is bordered on both sides by century-old maple trees and stone walls, with fields beyond them. We walk up a small hill, past the mailboxes of old friends, who I visited daily as a child, followed by a pack of dogs and God knows what else: Simon the Crow, Sylvester the Squirrel, Racquel the Racoon, all the family pets. I know all the nooks and crannies of the stone walls, the crooks in trees where I hid cigarettes and bags of pot throughout my adolescence. Framingham had the distinction of being the largest town in the country, but this area, known as Framingham Center, was an island within it, a land full of lunatics and magic. When I was about nine, wherever I walked in the neighborhood I was followed by Simon, my brother's pet crow brought home from a school project. Simon flew above me, bouncing from tree limb to telephone wire, cackling. And when I arrived at my destination he would dive bomb and land. If I was outside with friends, he'd hang around. If I went inside, he'd invite himself in. If that didn't work, he was off again on other adventures, "running errands." Simon was a busy crow. When he wasn't tagging along with one of us, he had his own friends, and his own routes. It seemed everyone knew him.

When, after a year or so, Simon disappeared, the local newspaper featured a story, "No Joy on Winch Street, Simon Is Gone." The reporter interviewed everyone in the neighborhood, who recounted Simon stories. The crow had made friends with the construction crew that was building a house down the road, the old lady across the street, and various others. He played games with people: hiding nails, interrupting family religious ceremonies, stealing berries. One of the more famous stories, not included in the newspaper, was the afternoon Bob ran into the house yelling that Simon was being attacked by a shrike. We all ran outside and on the top of the big oak tree was Simon being dive bombed. Bob got the 12 gauge shotgun and plugged the shrike as it and the crow swooped through the tree. The shrike was just behind the crow. Bob was standing in the road. It was a magnificent shot. Then in a fit of hatred Bob proceeded to squash its squirming remains into the road with the butt of the gun. (He told me later that nobody screws with his bird.) Meanwhile the crow flew back into the tree and Mother, dressed in a sensational silk tiger print jumpsuit, began climbing the tree shrieking. I stood under the tree as she climbed, holding onto her drink, smelling gin swirling around in a recycled peanut butter jar, ice tinkling. In the midst of all of this, a very proper neighborhood family we called the BeCrankies bicycled by, and true to her role, Mother hung by her knees and growled at them. The finale was the tree company arriving with a bucket to save Mother.

After the newspaper story ran and there was still no word and it seemed Simon was truly gone, Mother got bombed and kept calling her good friend in the police department, Officer Mahoney, to try to convince him to send out more patrol cars.

"Jesus Christ, Barbara," Mahoney apparently said, "I've done everything I can. In fact, I have personally talked to every fucking crow in this town and not one will admit to knowing you."

Not one of us escaped my mother's love for animals. Not even Bob, who acted so tough, and seemed so indifferent.

I turn to Dad one afternoon as we walk. "Do you remember Simon?"

"How could I forget," he laughs, and howls and repeats the Mahoney comment shaking his head. "That fucking crow! 'Barbara, I have talked to every crow in this town. . . .' Ha!"

The road's pavement is packed with millions of tiny pebbles and stones, rounded and worn by time. One afternoon, Dad and I stop at the top of a hill and admire a neighbor's barn, a tall, red beauty with enormous beams and planks. I spent endless afternoons there as a kid and teenager, brushing horses and cleaning tack with all my neighbor pals, girls with big bottoms who rode horses and got stoned.

We turn into the grassy drive to the barn, past an enormous elm tree and see that the huge door is open. Inside, a slew of dead animals hang from the ceiling, and a group of strangers, men with guns, mill about. In the driveway is a truck with guns hung on the back.

"Who the hell is this?" Dad asks under his breath.

"Those are coyotes, Dad. They're killing coyotes? I didn't even know there were coyotes here."

"Oh yeah," he says, "everywhere. We've seen them in the field. That and the deer."

A young man walks out. He is blond, in his early thirties, dressed in jeans and a T-shirt. "Hello, Mr. Montgomery," he says.

"Hello," Dad says, searching his face. "I'm sorry, I don't remember your name."

"Chris," the kid says, "The florist . . . Roz and Lenny's . . ."

"Grandson? That's right. How are you, Chris?"

Dad shifts uncomfortably but with enthusiasm. He lifts his shoulders and drops them in a quick motion and then purses his lips.

They spend the next few minutes talking about guns. I'm amazed that my father knows anything about them.

"Yeah, I used to like guns," he tells me as we walk away. "I had guns, my father's guns. You know your grandmother's father, Grandpa Coggin, was a big hunter. Anyway, when I married your mother, I got rid of them. Took them all to the cops."

On these walks, my father tells me more stories, or parts of them. Many I fill in later by talking to Lael or Bob, Dad's brothers, or Mom. When I do, I sometimes hear again about a man I never knew, a man who wanted to learn how to fly, a man who got into Harvard but couldn't go because he didn't receive enough scholarship money, a man who later dreamt of going to Harvard Business School.

"How come you didn't?"

"By then, the war came and I married your mother . . ."

"And then?"

"Who the hell knows, Lee. Life happened! I guess! Life! Happened! Watch out! It will get you, too."

He was right, but he could never imagine exactly how life had happened for me, and God knows I could never tell him.

❧

This is how the LSD goes into the eye, my boyfriend John (not his real name) instructed. The year was 1974; the place was my bedroom in my parents' home. John was a rich kid from outside New York City, spoke like his molars were glued together, and was my first true love. He reached into his pocket, unwrapped a little piece of paper that held all these tiny clear squares of LSD. He took his index finger ever so gently, licked it, and picked up a tiny translucent square and held it out for me to look at. "Here, watch," he said. "It's not a big deal."

Place the small pane, translucent, opaque, like a little window the size of a pinky fingernail. . . . Carefully balance the XX mg of vision on the tip of your finger. Use a finger of your other hand to pull back the eyelid. Slip the LSD in your eye. Hold the lid of the eye down until dissolved, and absorbed by the tiny vessels in your instrument of vision. R e g a r d e z. Witness! Watch!

He smiled. He was still dressed in part of his school uniform, a blue blazer. His long hair hung down no further than the frayed collar of his red and white striped dress shirt, according to school rules. But below the waist, he fell apart. His ratty Levis had holes at the knees and he wore beat-up hiking boots, his heavy woolen socks bunched up around his ankles.

I carefully licked my index finger and stuck it into the pile of little clear squares, like tiny windows of rock candy, and followed his instructions. Afterwards we kissed, and then sat on the floor smoking cigarettes through the open window, waiting for something to happen. When I felt the speed kick in, and glittery trails of light fell from the street lamps outside, we walked downstairs, through the living room, past Mom and Dad.

"Hey Pop," I said. "We're going. . . ."

My Dad's face melted, and as I passed by Mother passed out on the living room couch I could feel the room breathing. *Where were we? Life! Like inside some fucking movie.*

We walked outside into the darkness and slipped between the fence rails to the field. The ground was covered with snow, and as we walked, Happy followed us. I stopped, put my hand out and he nibbled it, and then I climbed up and hung my body over him. John did the same and we hung there, ears to the pony's stomach, listening to the pony breathe.

John used to joke that the pony talked, and had an uncanny ability to predict shooting stars. That night we sat and waited. I climbed underneath Happy and sitting on the ground placed my hand on his heart. *John? Where is the pony heart? Can you actually feel a pony's heart beat? Have you ever tried?*

Both Lael and Bob, who, as far as I know, weren't big

druggies like me, went to private schools. I too was supposed to go to a prep school as a day student starting in seventh grade. It was the same school that my mother, her sister Beverly, and Lael had attended: Dana Hall. But on the day I was to go, I refused. I was terrified. An all-girls school? Uniforms? Blek. I wanted to be able to hang out with all my friends and ride horses.

After a few more years in public school, I flunked some courses. It proved to be a smart move because it got everyone's attention. They pulled me out of public school, hired tutors, and sent me to a progressive new girls' school connected to St. Mark's, which was an old-fashioned Episcopal boys boarding school two towns over. Thankfully, the Southborough School was a little different. It was billed as an experiment, and full of wonderful, smart faculty who never once talked to me about my mother, but nevertheless knew enough to reach out to me. They saved my life.

After being tutored, I excelled at math. I had a high aptitude for chemistry. I liked to write for the newspaper, but preferred the seriousness of science. It brought me over to classes at the boys' school, and I loved boys! It also seemed to impress people, especially my father, who laughed proudly. Who would have thought, he would say, shaking his head. You and that math!

What wasn't readily obvious was that drugs were plentiful at St. Mark's. Within the year, I was drinking coffee, smoking cigarettes, and doing LSD, while simultaneously acing math, dissecting frogs, and reading Melville, Salinger, Porter, and Fitzgerald, and Zola and Colette in French.

The two schools were located a few miles apart, surrounded and separated by farmland. On the girls' school side was an enormous meadow bordered by dairy farms. On the St. Mark's side, closer to town, across the street from the actual school, a dirt road meandered by two skating ponds, each bordered by a stone skate house, and ended in perfectly manicured playing fields. Further beyond was the girls' field and a strip of woods. A year before the girls' school came, John and his friends spent weeks building a log cabin into the side of a hill. They worked at night, chopping down trees, and pulling logs. They built a fireplace, and even dug another room into the back. They called it Gramma's, in reference to: "Over the river and through the woods to Grandmother's house we go . . ."

And so we did go, almost daily, meeting in the field, following little paths through the woods to the cabin that allowed us to create another world. We had our own backwards language that the boys had invented: *Oeeee ew eb ginippirt. Woh tuoba a ytrap lwob. The Lapsta, Why did ya have to be such a tnuc ecaf.* And one enterprising boy even knew how to sing the Beatles' "Yesterday" backwards, and did so faithfully. We all had secrets, some more disturbing than others, but for that time we were able to leave them behind for Gramma's, a wonderful world far away from the real one that would eventually separate us.

Southborough School and St. Mark's had classes six days a week, with half days on Wednesdays and Saturdays. On Wednesday afternoons during my junior year, I often packed a picnic, a few blankets, and met John in the middle of the woods to have sex. Every few months, we'd drive my 1967 Chevy Nova II into Cambridge with other boys from St. Mark's to buy drugs at Harvard. We'd meet up with a boy we called Loose Wrongway Hemp who lived in Dunster

House. And the boys would buy pot, hashish, hash oil, and LSD, and transport it back to St. Mark's where they distributed it to all of their friends.

John was older, and graduated the year before me. The following year, he moved to Switzerland to go to school. I concocted a scheme to join him for the spring term of my senior year. In the meantime, my best friend Sally (not her real name), another day student, and I continued the tripping tradition. We took LSD and walked to the pizza store about two miles away from my parents' home. We called it the pizza journey. We'd walk arm in arm all through the neighborhoods, stopping outside people's houses to watch their lives unfold through their windows. We had many philosophies about life, and about God especially.

What do you remember? I ask her.

Only two hundred and fifty hits of purple microdot falling out in Ms. Palmer's (not her real name) *Duster.*

The theory, Sal, theories we had.

Which ones, she said. *We had many.*

Do you remember the one about living in one of those plastic snowballs? We lived in that perfect little town. Do you remember the one about the music?

Besides visiting Bobby and Susan and holiday dinners at Lael's when she was living in a nearby town, I remember very little about my home life during high school, and practically nothing about my mother. My father showed up at every school function with my Grandmother Montgomery, who lived in Southborough. I was always happy to see them, but shared nothing of myself except what I thought Dad might have wanted to hear.

By the time I moved to Lugano, Switzerland, John had fallen in love with someone else. Fifteen years after that, after struggling with severe depression and alcoholism, he blew his brains out. I'll never understand it because if we had made predictions, surely we'd have thought I'd be the one to do such a thing. He was slumming with me. His grandmother owned half of a block on Park Avenue. His father went to Harvard. He grew up in Bedford Hills. And who was I? Nobody: just a messy, stupid girl, daughter of an alcoholic mother. And at the time, as far as I knew, Mother was the only one in the world.

Not one person in my family liked John, and I think it's to their credit that I never knew that until he was long gone. Sadly, he wouldn't be the only suicide close to me. Almost all my former boyfriends are now dead. And many of the people whom I grew up with are also dead. My first boyfriend, Quentin, who I went steady with from the age of six to twelve, was found dead. It was ruled a suicide but his family thought he was murdered. The first boy I kissed died in a motorcycle crash. The man who took my virginity was murdered. Of our neighbors, Mrs. Goodwin hung herself; Dr. Sniffen shot himself; Sam may have overdosed; Billy wrapped himself around a tree. Timmy gassed himself in his VW. Jimmy overdosed. And remember our friends, the lunatics? They offed themselves, too.

9

THANKSGIVING

November 1998
Framingham, Massachusetts

When Pop naps today, he must dream about his fingers because they wiggle wildly in his lap as if they are playing a trumpet or milking a cow. He has told me about milking his father's dairy cows, about chapped hands and ice-cold cow teats at his family's farm in northern Massachusetts. How he hated all that. I don't know when hatred shifted into longing but he now talks sweetly of his father's barn. I have seen photographs of it, and other photos from Pop's childhood, and have often wondered what images Pop carries around in his head: an old truck piled with hay where he stands surrounded by friends and brothers with pitchforks, his old man standing in the doorway, and the melting water of an early snow. Because the photos are black-and-white, when I look at them, I paint in the autumn colors from the shadows and shades of gray of the trees.

The Montgomerys are old New Englanders. The Montgomery name is Scottish, but our forebearer Robert Mont-gomery, who died in Maine in 1758, was a linen weaver from Ireland. One of Robert's sons was a ship captain. The others were seamen. Many of them were lost at sea, according to Great Aunt Molly's genealogy. What they were trading we don't know—sugar and spices? Uncle Dick, Pop's younger brother, who has a flair for drama, insisted they were running rum and slaves, but Dad never said so. The others, who made their livings as farmers, carpenters, and locomotive engineers, as well as the sailors, are buried by the old shipyard in Booth-bay Harbor, Maine. My great grandmother's family, who migrated from New Brunswick and the Maritime Provinces, were thought to be Tories. But who knew? Pop rarely talked about his family. To him, they were a disappointing bunch. My father was the first in the family to go to college. Dick told me that their father was probably a manic-depressive, though again, Dad never said so. My grandfather was in constant financial trouble. His failures became my father's fuel, driving him to work hard in a solid engineering career, do the right thing, and take few risks. In other words, Pop was a major stick-in-the-mud, and his biggest extravagances seemed to be loud, drunk blondes, old MGs, and heirloom tomatoes.

When he wakes, his hand reaches for his stomach, pushing as he feels around. Like all tumors, his are hard like rocks, but if his hand could reach inside his belly, the cancer would feel slippery, slick to the touch. He pushes deeper.

"Dad, what are you doing?" I ask.

"Dying," he answers.

"What?"

"Not a fucking thing," he says.

"What?" I say again.

"I said 'not a fucking thing.'"

He pushes again. I lift my hand; I want to feel inside his stomach, too, but as I move closer, I just stand there, searching his face, pretending I am trying to remember something.

One morning, the house is in orbit because Pops can't poop. He sits in his easy chair downing mineral oil, a tablespoon an hour, looking miserable. No one knows what to do. The Kid circles, plays his clarinet, and Mother wanders aimlessly with her walker. She's getting over a bad cold and can't hear anything, so she yells.

"Don't yell at me," I say.

"I'm not yelling," she yells.

"Mother, you *are* yelling."

"I can't hear you. I feel like I'm far away down a tunnel and everyone is yelling at me."

Pop and I go for a drive to the bank, and though I am not nervous, I should be. He drives dangerously close to the shoulder of the road, almost swiping a few telephone poles. When we return, Mother sulks. Dad is getting too much attention.

"I would just like a bath," she says.

She tells me how to set up a chair next to the tub so that she can get in and out without crashing. This is my father's job, has been for years, ever since Mother broke her shoulder, pelvis, and knee. I look at my mother in the tub; her round soft body falls into a lovely heap in the bathwater.

We start to sing an old favorite, "I'm Feeling Sorry for Myself." We rewrite the lyrics as we sing, to fit our circumstances.

I'm as blue as blue can be.
My man got cancer on me.
I'd go out and end it all,
but forty-four floors is a terrible fall.
I'm feeling sorry for myself.

Mother actually knows how to sing. After she dropped out of Yale Drama School, she did radio, made a record, and sang with Billie Holiday's trumpet player. We have sung together for years, often teasing my father in our songs.

Hey, honey, you got any money,
That's all I want to know.

And for the days when we were feeling fat:

You can have her,
I don't want her.
She's too fat for me.

Sitting in the bathtub, Mother pulls out her best Judy Garland showmanship. She throws her good arm to the side, and moving her head to the rhythm, turns her face toward the ceiling like a howling wolf.

I feel a song coming on.

I laugh. It's hard to believe that she was my age when she would show up at the grocery store looking like a movie star: costumed in white jodhpurs and long dungaree jackets with her dyed platinum blond hair styled in a "pageboy" like Katherine Hepburn's in *Philadelphia Story*. Her sidesaddle riding outfits were even more spectacular: bare feet and black satin strapless evening gowns. In those days, she would haul out her long white evening gloves and smoke cigarettes in cigarette holders.

One of Bob's best friends, Frank, once told her that there was a rumor that she waited for the town to shut down at night and then stripped off her clothes, saddled up her horse sidesaddle and galloped around peoples' lawns, jumping over their hedges. I like this story, though I doubt it is true. Generations of my parents' families were farmers and sailors, and we still rose and fell with the sun. It seems to be genetic. If Mother ever stayed up late, she played her concerto on her baby grand piano, pounding out her stormy composition through the night, a rumble of blue notes, while her family tried to sleep.

Sleepy-eyed, we would all take turns trying to get her to stop. *Dad, tell her to stop. Mother stop. Barbara stop. Mom! Stop!*

"I don't like the word drunk," she told me one afternoon. "I prefer lush. It has a nice ring. Lush. Lush. Lush."

I used to visit all the gay places, she begins to sing now.

Those come what may places . . . I add.

And then together: *where one relaxes on the axis of the wheel of life . . . to get the feel of life . . . from jazz to cocktails . . .*

I will never be able to explain my mother, but I will most likely spend my life trying. She is the rock in the road that I navigate around. She is this, and then she is that. She is great fodder for outrageous stories, though there is another side. How do you explain that your mother drinks gin and tonics for breakfast? You don't.

How do you explain the behavior of your father, who stood stoically by this insanity? You cannot.

How can you explain yourself? Impossible.

People ask, *Aren't you angry with your father, too?* The answer is yes and also no.

At some point, my life becomes a hunt for theories to save me. To save us no less! To save Mother from herself. To save me from humiliation. Lael is a developmental psychologist and spends part of her days trying to understand what plagues our mother. Bob is a controls engineer, and becomes an expert at analyzing and controlling the real world. I am a writer, who makes a career as an editor, someone who helps other people tell their stories, mine too complicated for me to decipher.

My family has been its own lifelong conundrum, and the engine that fuels my exile. We always came up with numerous theories about addiction, but we were clueless about recovery. During the sixties and seventies, there were very few outlets for help for a family like ours, and even now when I sit in small rooms surrounded by people who are living in the nightmare of addicted sons and daughters, mothers and fathers, I see their complete helplessness. We can cure certain types of cancer, fly around the world at record speeds, send men to the moon, but it's impossible to get a drunk not to drink. After years of hoping and trying, we still stand around shaking our heads, looking at one another, and asking the same questions.

"What do we do about Mother?"

"What do you expect me to do," Pop always said. Why he ultimately chose to stand by her, locking everyone else out of their world, including us, is perplexing. Was it out of fear, loyalty, guilt, or love? His protection of her was their undoing. She could never get better; he could never leave.

My father's choices saddened me, because he lived in a world that I could no longer inhabit. It became easier for me to stop coming home, which is why it is remarkable that I stand here now. It has been at least thirty years since we have all slept under this roof together and yet we assemble. There is still love lurking in these shadows, regardless of the anger at how Mother's "illness" tore us apart, and the sadness about how it takes father dying to bring us back. It occurs to me at some point that it isn't until my father begins to die that I begin to live. Death is nonnegotiable; it's impossible for me to idealize our lives while looking through its lens.

But that afternoon with Mother, I am thinking about other things, namely that—amidst all the confusion, my restless searching—there is still beauty in what she has taught me. I remember little about our country's history, or cooking a Sunday roast, but I know, for example, how to make a lettuce Thanksgiving turkey for horses, mix a great martini, and sing all the songs of Judy Garland, even the medleys.

> *We're a couple of swells.*
> *We stay in the best hotels.*

And

> *You made me love you.*
> *I didn't want to do it.*

She hands me a washcloth.

"What?" I ask, holding it by a corner, and I repeat my favorite part to egg her on.

I'd go out and end it all, but forty-four floors is a terrible fall.
"Throw it."

"Mother, what are you talking about?"

"Your father throws it to see if he can hit . . ."

She points to a towel rung hung on the opposite wall over two sinks. I pull her up out of the bath and place a towel over her shoulders.

I'm feeling sorry for myself, she sings.

"Dad," I yell. "Come on in and throw the washcloth."

"I don't want to," he says. "I'm happy where I am."

"C'mon."

"I'm happy where I am."

So I throw it and mother watches wide-eyed as a child when I hit dead ringer.

"Score!" I yell.

"Monty, she hit it."

She stands with the towel on her shoulder and hobbles into the bedroom and we find Dad stretched out in his easy chair feigning sleep. I lie down on his side of the bed and watch them. Mother takes hours dressing. As she slips a jersey around her neck, her right arm threads her left arm through a sleeve. She throws her pants on the floor and steps into them. With the fabric bunched around her ankles, she takes a break, sips her martini, and holding the gin in her mouth, studies my father. I wonder what she thinks about. "Old fella," she says. She closes her eyes for an instant, and I imagine she is remembering something sweet, perhaps the time she told me about when her father drove them in his Plymouth from New Hampshire to Boston. Her father smoked a big stinky cigar as he drove so she rolled down the windows even though it was the middle of February. Pop sat next to her in the back seat, and because she said she was freezing, he pulled her close. He then kissed her sweetly on the lips. A first kiss. They were eighteen.

According to family lore, Pop was my mother's sister Beverly's boyfriend first. They met one summer in the middle of the Squam Lake where both families had summer homes. Mom and Beverly had a trick to meet boys. They drove their father's Chris Craft into the middle of the lake, turned the engine off, and pulling off the cover of the inboard motor, pretended something was broken. Invariably a boatload of boys would stop and offer to help. Before they knew it the Begole girls had a new season of suitors, of which Pop was one.

Sixty years later, I watch them both and think about the length of time they've spent together. Three years ago on their fiftieth anniversary, Pop kept saying, "Fifty years! Do you have any idea of how many days that is? Eighteen thousand two hundred and fifty!"

I count them again now: 19,345 days, 464,280 hours, 27,856,800 minutes, and countless breaths—more than 557 million, if you estimate that we take an average of 20 breaths per minute.

I watch his chest rise and fall. Not one of us can imagine what busies itself under his skin. Those few crazy cells, made from stomach and ducts, are moving through his system without rest. They are dividing madly in the spaces where his organs once were, growing exponentially in the little pocket of stomach that's left.

My mom looks at her ring finger. His wedding band is back on her finger, steadied by other small keeper rings. She places two fingers on the gold band and twists it around.

"Hey, Mom," I ask. "Did you and Dad ever dance?"

She looks at him. Her eyes grow round and sad.

"Monty," she says. "Monty."

She says it again and again, each time louder and louder until he finally opens an eye.

"What?" he says.

She brings up a finger and bites the edge of a cuticle.

"Did we ever dance? Do you remember?"

He smiles. "Hell, yes. Once. A long time ago."

"When," she asks.

"Oh, Christ, Barbara, I don't know," he says. "At our wedding, I suppose."

My mother looks so sad. "Do you remember all the birds?" she turns to me. "Do you?"

I nod. When I was young, Mom and I often banded together on search and rescue missions to save the lives of critters—usually half-eaten baby bunnies or half-baked baby birds who'd fallen out of their nest. Each morning when the infirmary was operational, we nervously peeked under the towels covering our patients' cages to see if they'd lived through the night.

"This is what I think of when I wake up next to your father," she tells me. "I have to turn over and lift up the towel to see if he made it through the night."

A week before Thanksgiving, my father well on the mend, I leave Boston at four in the morning. First, I wake and smooch my parents while they still lie sleepily in their bed. Then, after climbing into a limousine, I ride through a cold darkness to the plane. I know they are relieved to have me gone. It is probably a matter of hours before they pull down all my charts pinned up in the kitchen about what my father should eat, each box containing the proper number of calories for small meals evenly divided throughout the day. The notebooks I've started for him to track his meals end the moment I leave. And though they don't tell me for many months, at some point soon after I go away, they both pad into the kitchen with a wastebasket by one of their sides and throw away all the food Lael, Bob, and I have bought: the four varieties of ice cream, the yogurt and tofu and soybeans, the vitamins and calorie boosters, the half-and-half and whole milk, the vitamins, the flaxseed oil, the Ensure, the Met-Rx.

"I hate that stuff," Dad yells at me months later. "Don't you buy it. I won't eat it. I'll throw it away!"

His anger surprises me. Pop's coping method is typically to shut down and vanish. I've rarely seen him angry and raising his voice.

While Lael and I are away, we send books about cancer, about survival, about fighting back, about shark cartilage and choices and healing, all of which go unread. My father tells us about a constant pain, the deep, gnawing ache of a stomach departed. We have all been harboring the hope that he will live for years, but as the months click by and he doesn't rally, the hope moves and shifts. It moves from "years" to "a year." Then we hope for a summer. I find myself wishing he would feel better, have one more summer, and then roll over and die peacefully and swiftly.

I call once a day, often more, to get updates from Mom, and hear Dad's voice, hoping for good news. I do all the wrong things. I drill them on his diet, again suggesting soybeans, *anything* to keep him from dropping from my sight. *Little meals. Don't lie down. Vitamins. Essential fatty acids. Whole dairy products. Not skim. Pie? Pasta? What laxative? Did you call the nutritionist? Don't use enemas. Call the doctor. Are you walking?*

Lael, Bob, and I conspire behind our parents' backs, checking with doctors and helpers to see if Dad is eating. After Lael and I call Mom and Dad, we call each other, then call Bob, then call each other again. Bob is the only one actually in Boston, and being more *laissez-faire* in general, he grows annoyed with us for whooping everyone up into an anxious fit from the West Coast. But we do it anyway. Daily, in a nervous flutter, nagged by the guilt over our physical distance. We hen and we peck. I might be worse than Lael, falling apart when my father's voice is weak or when he tells me his stomach hurts. I hold onto the idea of saving him even though, each day, as our conversations grow shorter, because he is tired and in pain and doesn't feel like talking, our distance widens, and the more emptiness I feel.

Still, these are several months, November, December, January, and most of February, when I believe he might make it. If he'd only gain weight. If he'd only eat many small meals. If he'd only eat vitamins, get more exercise . . .

Bob drives Dad in and out of Boston and reports back, typically sharing good news, but when I talk to Dad, he reports only bad news. "My stomach hurts," Dad says. "My stomach is killing me."

This is a bad year for cancer. Six months earlier, my husband Tom's mother is diagnosed with breast cancer. A month later, his younger brother Terrance's wife Mary, who is thirty-nine, is diagnosed with metastatic lung cancer. By December, we have three family members battling cancer. After years of doing nothing with my biology degree, I have suddenly found a use for my science background and the years I spent working as a research assistant. (Coincidentally, one job was in immunology at Harvard, two doors down from where my father was later treated.) I know enough about the big words to become a lay expert. My mother-in-law and I establish daily phone updates, comparing treatment notes for her, Mary, and my Dad. We become fluent in cancer lingo, side effects, clinical trials, chemo regimes, morphine patches, pumps, and radiation.

"Think shrink," Mary tells me on the phone when she hears about my father. She is riddled with cancer in every part of her body, from lung to brain to bone. She weighs ninety pounds—but what a helluva ninety pounds.

"Think shrink!" she says, laughing.

It is December, a few weeks before Christmas, about the time my father sees his oncologist as well as a radiologist for his first follow-up visit to find out about other treatment options.

December 11, 1998

Mr. Robert Montgomery is a 76-year-old gentleman s/p resection of a gastric adenocarcinoma who presents today for a follow-up visit. He is seen in conjunction with Dr. Harvey Mamon of Radiation Oncology.

Mr. Montgomery was initially evaluated at the Dana-Farber Cancer Institute on 10/21/98, at which time recommendation was made for resection of his gastric adenocarcinoma. Mr. Montgomery did in fact undergo resection with Dr. Osteen on 10/27/98. He underwent subtotal gastrectomy. At the time of the operation, he was found to have 15 cm poorly differentiated adenocarcinoma, diffuse type with signet ring fea-tures. The tumor was found to be adherent to multiple intra-abdominal structures, including the tail of the pancreas, the spleen, as well as the crura of the diaphragm. Malignant lymph nodes were noted along the splenic artery. Three perigastric lymph nodes were positive and the proximal resection margin was also positive for tumor. Tumor was noted in the peripan-creatic and parisplenic adipose tissue.

In the case of the patient, extensive disease was found at the time of the surgery and it is unlikely that additional chemo/radiation at this time would be curative. Such therapy may also result in significant toxicity in this elderly gentle-man. It was therefore our recommendation that Mr. Mont-gomery undergo no further adjuvant therapy at this time.

That same day, across the continent, I am Christmas and birthday shopping for my dad in the Made in Oregon store. I drift for hours, poking at Oregon treasures, smoked salmon and huckleberry jams, and then lap back to the land of Pendleton, where all the shirts hang, placing my hands on the itchy wool, feeling the leather elbow pads, the crosshatch leather buttons. Throughout my life, my father has worn these woolen shirts at holidays: the red, the blue, this plaid, that green. I finger the shirts like treasures, watching old scenes in my head, smelling Old Spice, hearing a hoot or two while savoring the sight of my father's freshly shaven face above a holiday dinner. With the smell of cigarette tobacco in my hair, I replay the Christmas stories he tells about me. Christmas as a child I dutifully left Santa a gin and tonic in a mayonnaise jar with a lid, alongside goodies for the reindeer. I would awake in the middle of the night to open all my presents and, after seeing what I got, wrap them back up.

"Ha! A con you are," my father says with a laugh. "A sneaky thing!"

A saleslady finds me sitting on the floor of the store with my hand in my mouth.

"Is there anything I can help you with?" she asks.

I turn to her, lost in reverie.

"I was looking for something in green," I say, and then hear a strange moan come from the center of my chest.

⚮

At the end of January, at just forty years old, Mary is dead. Tom travels to Connecticut to help Terrance with the funeral arrangements. Tom's eighty-year-old father flies up from the Byrnes' home in Florida and though Tom's mother is fine, she is still undergoing chemo and radiation so stays home, which means we're still on the phone.

In Boston, a few hundred miles north from Tom's family's sad days in Connecticut, Dad has a check-up. I am in Portland and I wait all day for my parents' call, spending most of the afternoon on the floor of my office, staring out the window at the telephone wires, the rain, pieces of sky-high cedar trees. The phone rings.

"It's back," Mother says.

"Let me talk to Dad."

"Dad?"

"Yes."

"What did they say?"

He begins to reel off the locations of the tumors—

according to him, only three. With the exception of the one in his stomach, as far as I can tell they live in vague places, hard to visualize or locate.

"Bob will fax you the clinical trial," he asks.

"Okay," I say. "What do you think?"

"Looks good, I guess?" he says. "Fifty percent . . . I don't know what to think, but I can tell you this. After reading the side effects, I want to find the nearest apple tree to hang myself."

In the old days, Dad wanted to find an apple tree to sit under to drink beer.

Bob faxes me information about the clinical trial:

You have been invited to participate in this research study. You have esophageal or gastric (stomach) cancer that cannot be removed by surgery. There is no standard treatment, which could cure you at this point. The three anticancer drugs being used in this study have all been shown individually to have activity against esophageal and gastric cancer. This study, however, is investigational. Approximately 32 patients will participate in this study.

If you decide to take part in this study, you will receive cisplatin and doxorubicin once every three weeks. These anticancer drugs will be given intravenously (by vein) in the outpatient clinic. The actual time receiving these drugs will take approximately one hour; however you will also receive extra intravenous fluids (water with salt) before and after the chemotherapy, so that the total amount of time you will be in the clinic will be approximately 4 hours. In addition to the cisplatin and doxorubicin every three weeks, you will receive the anticancer drug 5-fluorouracil which will be given intravenously as a continu-

ous infusion for the duration of the study. In order to do this you will have a small pump that you can carry with you (usually on your belt or shoulder). This pump contains . . .

∽

Bob calls the doctors and I scour the Internet all that day, and a day later we reconvene on a conference call: Bob in Boston, Lael in San Diego, me in Portland.

"It's terminal," Bob says.

"What does that mean?" Lael asks.

"If he doesn't do treatment or doesn't respond to treatment, maybe a month."

"Otherwise?" Lael asks.

"Six to nine," Bob says. "Maybe."

"What does Smiling Bob say?" I ask.

"A disappointing recurrence," Bob says. "He was hoping for a year."

Bob begins to read his notes, and mentions tumors in the liver and lung.

"I haven't heard that," I say. "Where does he get that Dad has tumors in the liver and lung? The oncologist didn't say so."

"Beats me," Bob says. "He was looking at the CAT scans. It's moving fast."

"What?" Lael asks.

"The cancer, you ditz," I say. "What about etoposide?"

"I forgot to ask," Bob says.

"What about Dad?" Lael asks.

"The doctor thinks Dad knows what he wants to do," Bob says. "Some people have a slow process of accepting."

"That's an understatement," Lael says. "What do we do?"

"Nothing," Bob says. "We go along with it. They have social workers who can help. They restage at six weeks."

"What does that mean?" Lael asks.

"To see if the chemo works," I say.

"If it doesn't?" Lael asks.

"Who knows?" Bob says. "They try something else."

"Some of the studies have results," Bob says. "I think this is the best one."

"What about intravenous feeding so he can gain weight?" I ask.

"I forgot what he said," Bob says.

"Schedule," I say. "I'll be there for the first ten days of March."

"I'll be there on the eighth," Lael says.

"I'll take the beginning of April," Bob says.

Dad's visits are weekly, but chemo infusions are scheduled for every three weeks.

We make our schedules. We think we have it covered.

Later that day, I am sitting on the floor again, staring at the longest, darkest sky ever, and thinking about my father. No stomach. No spleen, and yet he worsens. When I talk to him on the phone, I know he sits in his easy chair and watches the rain drip from the gutters out front. Behind him, his old field is wet and brown. No snow. The ground begins to loosen from winter's hold.

He must think of asking the oncologist—*What about the other participants? What do you know about the others?*—but I imagine he can't find the courage so instead watches the oncologist smile and leave the room to wander the tiny hallways on the top floor of the cancer center, his white coat billowing. Out of habit, his index finger separates from the others and points down at nothing. The doctor cannot say *everyone dies here* so he says nothing.

February 23, 1999

Mr. Robert Montgomery returns today for a follow up of his gastric cancer. He was seen last week at which time we noted he was developing progressive cachexia and anorexia since his surgery three months ago. Given the concern for the development of metastatic disease, he has undergone re-staging.

And it goes on to itemize what they saw in Pop's CAT scan:

Evidence of new metastatic disease. Multiple small nodular opacities. A moderate pericardial effusion. A destructive lower left rib lesion. A 6 x 7 cm liver mass. Retroperitoneal lymphadenopathy.

And then it says:

I discussed the results of the CAT scan with Mr. Montgomery and his son today. My recommendation was for initiation of systemic chemotherapy with the hope of shrinking the tumors and palliating some of the symptoms. Mr. Montgomery is clearly interested in pursuing such therapy. We will go ahead and obtain a chest CAT scan for complete staging purposes and also schedule Mr. Montgomery for a port-a-catheter placement. He will return following these procedures for initiation of treatment.

10

LONG WINTER

February 1999
Portland, Oregon

Can we talk about rain? My father is dying, and here in Oregon, the rain does not stop. I look outside one day in March, after more than one hundred days of rain, and think, we're looking at another four months of *what?*

Rain.

That means that of the three hundred days until the turn of the millennium, it will rain for at least two hundred.

Whereas in most parts of the country, there seems to be an agreement about what rain is, in Oregon rain means something else entirely. Here they don't mean *rainrain go away, pitter patter, rain for a few days,* they mean *Rain, WOW! Rain, really! Rain forever! Rain, no foolin'!*

"It's like a comic strip," Lael says. She lives surrounded by a circle of mountains she can actually see. "I mean the rest of the country is clear as a bell and there is that little pulsating cloud up there in the corner of the weather map. Does it ever go away?"

"I don't think so," I say.

"Beautiful day," Mom and Dad say. "What's about you, or dare we ask?"

"The same," I say. "Rain. Rain today. Rain tomorrow. Rain forever."

I begin to count days. After twenty, it's difficult not to notice the wide array of rain and fixate on the possibilities for brief respite. For instance, a nuisance rain is expected, one local weather forecaster reports as I see another five days of cartoon clouds in front of a beating sun. There is the possibility of a sun break on Thursday. There may be a blue burst on Saturday.

I chart them all on my calendar so I can be sure to be strategically stationed by a window to get a pittance of sun. A burst means some clear sky but not necessarily sun. A moment is comprised of a sixty-second interval of sun, and they sometimes occur quite frequently, and sometimes consecutively. After three moments they graduate to a break. Whatever. Clear skies disappear as quickly as they appear. Bottom line is I can't wait to get out of here. I actually look forward to climbing on the airplane and going east. I long to fly above the clouds, above the rain.

I've only been in Oregon for six months and I hate it. I also hate my husband. He is on the road all the time and when he is home he is crabby and blathers nonstop about business issues. I am completely homesick for our old home of Topanga Canyon in the mountains outside of Los Angeles. I miss the shenanigans of LA. I miss the bad facelifts and fake tits, the movie deals, the flawless porcelain teeth, and the fact that, after a glass of chardonnay, *everyone* is a writer.

I was the editor of the town newspaper, and everyone from the homeless to the sheriff and county politicians stopped by the office to catch me up on the politics and gossip: land use issues in the Santa Monica Mountains, the corrupt building department, the fate of the day laborers, septic systems in Malibu; who's screwing who. I miss them all. I miss Murphy, the dapper drunk who lived under the palm tree across the street, and who wanted to be a reporter. I miss the grocer, the checkout guys from Pakistan who I called the Blahblahs because they were always speaking Urdu and it sounded like blahblahblah. I miss Shelby, my homeless "assistant" who lived in a camper in the back parking lot and who I had to fire because he was dealing coke out of the front office. I miss Blackie, the town philosopher, who liked to lecture me about the virtues of Mexican Therapy (smoking marijuana) and his philosophy on thin women—the thinner, the meaner. I miss Dick Sherman, a squat man with white hair cut in a Prince Valiant style, and his wonderfully filthy jokes. Dick owned Topanga Excavation, a septic company, and knew every water pipe from Santa Monica Canyon to Point Dume, and often joked about writing a column called *What's the Poop?* I miss all the "creekers"—the homeless drunks and ex-roadies, the vets, the groupies, and drug addicts—who hang around the town center, hurrying in and out of my office telling perfectly ridiculous stories. I miss the dreamland of LA, a place where no one ever grows old, a town where almost anything is possible. Always. Forever.

In Oregon, where it rains nonstop, there's no such thing

as bad weather, only bad clothing. The positivity is nau-
seating. Everyone is healthy, and everyone recycles. At first
I know no one who smokes, swears, or drinks martinis.
Everyone is on good behavior. They ride bicycles in the
rain. They use biodiesel and are responsible, ethical, moral,
and incredibly boring. Their favorite expression is *No
worries, no dramas.* No fun. Lael calls them the *Nike Do-It*
people.

And then there is this: Over and over throughout this
first year in Oregon, I am hardly there. When I am, it rains
nonstop. I fly back and forth to Boston, in and out of the
sky and the storm clouds, and look at my ailing father, real-
izing again and again: there is the possibility here of the
unimaginable. And then, I look at Mother, who is drunk
most of the time, and feel myself tumbling back into the
world I have spent a lifetime running from.

When I travel to Boston in March, it's the first time I have
seen the sun in months. I fly over the Cascade Mountains,
over Idaho and Montana and into Chicago, where I leave
one plane and find another, at the very end of a grand hallway full of busy, shiny people carrying black leather bags
and newspapers and cardboard boxes of deep dish pizza,
their luggage on wheels behind them. None of them seems
to have anything to do with where I came from or where I
am going. In the plane, I choose emergency exit row seating because I am a nervous flyer and being situated where I
can imagine the possibility of saving lives, mainly my own,
is a deep comfort.

When we take off again out of O'Hare, the strange shifting of gravity steals my breath. I turn to peer out the win-

dow over the big city of Chicago and, as I do, I hear my mother's voice singing, *Chicago, Chicago, that doddering town.* We fly and fly, over all the states in the center of the country and the North and the East, arriving in Boston after the sun has gone down. Floating over the harbor, the islands are indistinguishable in darkness, yet, *halleluia,* I can actually see the lights of Boston glitter below.

The airport shuttle service provides the same driver for the duration of my father's illness, an impish Irish man from Southie who has red, red hair, and dark, smiling eyes and who talks nonstop for the twenty-mile trip. Boston is in the thick of the Big Dig, the enormous reconfiguring of its roads, and every time I fly in or out of the city, new tunnels spit us out in unfamiliar places. This time we drive through upturned earth and slush and steel beams, cranes and bright lights with burly men in hard hats, smoking and yelling. We are in the center of the construction bedlam engineered toward easing traffic and the eternal nightmare of Boston's famous Southeast Expressway, usually called The Distress Way.

Rome wasn't built in a day, a billboard reads. *Give us a break.*

I laugh. Yankee humor. Cynical. Skeptical. The driver chats.

"Unbelievable," he says, waving his hand at his window, which frames a worker and a steel crane. "The corruption. Unbelievable!"

On these trips back and forth through fall, winter, and summer, to and from, back and forth, Brian the Driver talks nonstop about everything under the sun. The world. President Clinton. City politics. The friggin' mayor (*mayah*).

Architecture. Alcoholism. Living simply. God. The stock market. Nutrition. The Kennedys.

"Y'know what I mean?" he asks. "It's wicked." He shakes his head and looks at me through the rearview mirror.

His words wash by as the pilgrim hat of the Massachusetts Turnpike insignia comes into and out of view. As the cab drives from Boston through the 'burbs to Mom and Dad's house, I push my face up against the glass to watch the sky. Finally, a tollbooth and then onward through the darkness. We drive by the Town Common, the historical society, the cemetery on tree-lined streets, bare now with winter trees, under the railroad bridge. We pass the Webster house, allegedly built by an ancestor who made spinning wheels and founded Stanford University. A mile later, we zip up our driveway, which is angled at thirty degrees. I sign a credit card receipt and climb out. It's cold. Stars and a big fat moon light up the winter sky. I pull my bags on wheels and clump along, past the *click click* of the garden gate, the *whoppawhoppa* of the bags' plastic wheels against the brick. The lights have been left on in anticipation of my arrival and, as I trundle up the stairs, I imagine the moment they might have remembered to do this.

Monty, for Christ's sakes, lights!

I pull open the storm door and it pounds twice as it shuts behind me. Back and forth I go from the front porch into the house, pulling my bags into the kitchen. I walk down the lavender-carpeted hallway into my parents' room. My mother is sound asleep. Her face is rounder, her hair shorter; she has just turned seventy-eight. Next to her is my father, very thin, one hundred and twenty pounds on a good day. He sits up in bed.

"Hey there, Pops. How are you?"

"I'm not doing so good, Kid," he says.

He doesn't look at me when he says this, his shoulders move up and down once. He has a bit of food on his face and is fiddling with something in his hand. I sit on the edge of the bed and kiss him. He looks up, happy to see me, and I notice the plastic tubes of the portacatheter, hanging just under his shoulder, a system of tubes inserted in a vein to take the constant infusion of chemotherapy that will begin in a few days.

"Not doing so good, Kid," he says again.

I kiss him again.

"I'm so sorry, Dad."

I sit on the bed and hold onto his old root hands and will myself not to cry, banishing the wild alarm, the great weight of sadness at how thin he has grown, how ill he appears.

It is a dismal time here in New England, too, this March business. Brown earth is everywhere. At the bottom of the field, I can make out the edge of the wood in the moonlight, the top of trees brittle with winter decay.

I climb upstairs and begin to wander. The house is hot, too hot. The old cast-iron oil furnace burns overtime and the four upstairs bedrooms are cracking in the dry heat. I walk from room to room—the entire second floor is mine—and remember when all these rooms were full, thirty years ago. My brother's and sister's rooms were to the left of the stairs, my parents' and mine to the right. I walk by blanket chests and wall mirrors I used to talk to when I was a teenager trying to figure out who I was, why I was, or if I was at all. Standing in front of the mirror now, seeing shades of my grandmother in my own eyes, I hear my father's yells from years before. I had just graduated from college and was home for the summer, trying to figure out my next step.

"Put some clothes on," he bellowed. "For Christ's sakes, what are you? Some kind of a nudist?"

"Father darling," I told him then, "there is nothing wrong with the human body."

"Yeah. Yeah. Yeah. I don't give a damn, put some clothes on."

A lot had changed in the five years I had been away at college. One change was that my mother and father had both given up drinking. In the late seventies, Dad had been diagnosed with diabetes, so about a year before I returned home, they went on a big health kick. Dad lost a hundred pounds. Mom slimmed down and began buying horses and riding again.

I, of course, had changed, too. I had little use for clothes, for instance. When I first moved home, I wandered around without them, claiming they were too burdensome and that the Hanson boys who watched me paint the house or sunbathe nude while they hayed our field would just have to get over it—a comment that sent my father into a fury.

I also felt it was critical to touch and kiss everyone incessantly, which, even clothed, created great discomfort in a family that made it a habit to not touch anyone, ever. And as for biochemistry, the subject of my degree, past research jobs, and beginning graduate studies? I had no interest. I was moving to Paris to become a writer and a filmmaker with the French New Wave!

"Like hell," my father said as he turned and walked out of the room.

It was a bit of a miracle that I graduated from college since I had spent most of my college years on the West Coast, but such is the way of Antioch, where students study on campus for a few months and then take off to work. After six months at Antioch, I left for California where I stayed a year. My first job was classic Antioch. I was an assistant to a onetime scientologist now turned sociologist/hypnotist, who hypnotized fat people on how not to be fat. He paid me in pot. A year later, after working for a ceramicist in Mill Valley and a few veterinarians in San Francisco, I returned to Antioch for a year straight, only to take off again. And so it went. Back and forth. My last jaunt had been to Portland, Oregon, where I worked full-time for a year as a research assistant at the Oregon Health Science Center and took biochemistry courses at the state university.

I had taken a leave of absence from my job to return to Antioch for a term to finish my degree. Following graduation, I was planning to return to my job in Oregon and start preparing for medical school. Everyone was pleased. I seemed to be smart and responsible.

My only problem was I didn't want to study science. Not really. I did it because I thought it would please my Dad. Though I had given up drugs when I was eighteen, I was too confused emotionally to even begin to know who I was, so the easiest thing was to pretend to be someone else. For the five years of my college career, as I wandered the continent taking advanced placement science classes here and there, trying to be serious and scientific, I called my father repeatedly and begged for his permission to forget the whole thing.

"What are you going to do?" he asked.

"I don't know," I answered.

"Look, I am not going to send you to school to weave baskets."

"But, Dad, I hate physics. I don't get it."

"Study," he said.

"I want to go to Mexico," I said. "I want to learn Spanish."

"What you need to do is finish your degree and get yourself a job."

"But, Dad," I said. "I want to make movies."

"You heard me."

So, I finished my degree. On a beautiful summer day, my father sat in an audience of a few hundred people in the middle of nowhere Ohio. Antioch is not known for tradition, pomp, or formality of any kind, but chairs were assembled quaintly on the lawn under enormous oak trees. The stage was set, the podium was up, and after a few wonderful speakers (whose names neither Tom nor I can remember) the graduates' names were called. After moving through the reception line on the makeshift stage and receiving my diploma from the president, instead of following the others off the stage, I stopped to search out my father's location in the audience. Finding him I broke off from the crowd and walked down the aisle. I climbed over people and chairs until I reached him and then, with great gesture and aplomb, I curtsied and handed my diploma to him. At the time, I thought it was funny. I only meant to acknowledge his patience and investment, but as time has passed I've come to shrivel at the thought of embarrassing him, and how terribly misguided that gesture was.

It would take a few years after graduating from college to finally leave science, and a few more years after that to begin to figure out what I wanted. But my well-constructed façade began to unravel during my last term at Antioch. With the exception of finishing an independent study in the philosophy of science and a pharmacology class, for the first time since I was sixteen, I took no other science classes; only experimental film and video classes. I spent most of my last term trying to copy the film style of Carl Dreyer, shooting black-and-white movies of naked ladies eating lunch in abandoned college buildings, trying to make the science building shoot off like a rocket on 16 mm film, and editing *Artifact 80,* a yearbook, something unheard of at Antioch. I had also dumped my longtime boyfriend, a chemist who was working at MIT, to take up with a few young men, a ceramicist and a string of other artistic types, one of whom—a Frenchman, a photographer, filmmaker—happened to be a homosexual, too. We met in our film seminars. We studied Cahiers du Cinéma, watched experimental films and films of the French New Wave nonstop, smoked Gauloises, and argued about everything.

What BD didn't know was that by graduation, I had already quit my job in Oregon and planned to move back to Boston with my French friend. The plan was to mooch off the parents, save some dough, and move to Paris. I wanted to break it to the old man slowly. I thought I would return home first and have Alain follow a few weeks later for what we'd tell Mom and Dad would be only a few days.

Alain and I had concocted a fabulous scheme. We would import plastic birds from Marseille and sell them at beaches and other tourist spots around Boston. Alain had created a booming business in San Francisco a few years before and was convinced this was a certain road to riches. We would make some money, get married in order to get dual citizenship in France and the U.S., move to Paris, make films, and most importantly wear big hats.

When the birds arrived, we borrowed my mother's humongous blue Buick convertible and began our selling tours. We were arrested and fined at our first stop, Fanueil Hall in Boston, but not to be dissuaded, we carried on: the Cape, Newport, Rhode Island, North Shore. After a few weeks of bombing out everywhere, we knew we had to regroup. Maybe we needed to marry first so Alain could work in the States? We conspired and one night, Alain made a quiche dinner for Mom and Dad. Quiche was considered "new" cuisine so Pop sampled it cautiously, but was courteous. After dinner, Alain ceremoniously bent to his knees and asked my father's permission to marry me. My father began to choke and had to leave the room. Mother began to laugh so hard she spit out her food. Within a few days Mom and Dad made it known that Alain had to go, and I had to find myself a job.

Dad never really forgave me for that summer. Any time I mentioned Alain, he would always reply, "That bird!" And I know he must have found me more than infuriating, but, after that summer, rarely said so. I moved to Cambridge shortly afterwards, and worked everywhere and nowhere, back and forth between television and science, television and science, until I did eventually move to France. During those years, Dad said little unless my car got booted (again) or I used the credit card that he had given me for emergencies to shop at Ann Taylor. Instead, he began greeting any newly hatched plan with a wry smile, a distant look, a jingle of change in his pocket, a rocking on the soles of his shoes, as if to say, *Someday you'll know what I'm talking about, but on this day I don't have the energy to point out your utter lack of logic or practicality.*

11

CHEMOTHERAPY

March 1999
Framingham, Massachusetts

The moon spills a buttery light through the window of the bedroom I sleep in, which was my parents' bedroom when I was a child. Back then, I often slept with them. Afraid of dreams, of shadows, of bogeymen, I'd wake and walk down the hall to their room and climb into their bed, pushing my mother into the center or slipping in between them. There, in darkness, I'd listen to them breathe, lulled by the rhythm of their sleep. Now that we are all grown up or grown old, it's the same. In the early morning following the night of my arrival, I wander downstairs through the kitchen into their new bedroom to watch them sleep. They snore in unison. I climb into bed carefully, moving myself between them and turning on my stomach, I face my father. He opens a sleepy eye. His hand reaches for me. It settles on my head. My father pats my head, strokes my hair, and on the other side, I feel my mother's hand on my shoulder.

"You have such beautiful hair," my father says, as he has said for all of time. I am Tiny again, forever bound to these two souls as their youngest. I reach toward my father's stomach, now concave and bony with a magnificent, evil-looking scar. I let my hand rest in the air, palm down, a few inches off his stomach and make a magical grinding noise.

Be gone! Be gone!

My father's cancer doesn't answer back but keeps moving through belly, heart, liver, kidney, and lung. *Be gone! Be gone!*

He smiles sadly and I return my head to the pillow to rest and to savor the beauty of this long moment of us lying here as adults, lovingly patting one another like old monkeys, sad spectators, hoping for a miracle even though we are a family of nonbelievers. So much has happened between us and so little of it matters now. All I know is that I want to be here with my father. I do not want to leave his side.

I make them breakfast. Mom gets split pea soup and Dad crispy bacon and cornflakes with skim milk and strawberries. I ask Pops about the skim milk and he kindly tells me to bugger off. I look at his bony Biafran legs. "Dad, the calories might make a difference."

"I don't give a hoot," he yells. "I'm tired of people's advice. I will eat whatever I damn well please."

He slams drawers and cabinets and walks out of the room, mad and unsteady on his stick legs. My mother folds the dishtowel she is using as a napkin on her lap and gives me the eye as if to say, *Now do you see?*

It was on this trip that I named Dad "Thunder" and Mom "Lightning" for their belligerent, unpredictable behavior and incessant arguing. I also began reciting headlines about their murder.

"Elderly Couple Found Slain in Back Field," I yell as my father leaves the room. *"Youngest Daughter, Prime Suspect, on the Run!"*

Mother laughs.

"She thought she was just coming home to help," I continue loud enough so my father will hear me, *"but her father's stubbornness drove her to MURDER!"*

"Don't," my mother says, patting the tears of laughter streaming down her face with a napkin. "Please."

"Monty," she yells, as she pulls herself up onto the walker and hobbles out of the room. "Monty! Damn you!"

And in the distance, I hear, "Barb-rrra will you please just get off my back? I will not . . . ."

"And," I continue to the empty room, now more dramatic monologue than news story, *"she was destined to think of them whenever she heard that boom and crack in the night!"*

∞

It is afternoon, and my father reads in a chair. Behind him is a glass room where a hot tub overlooks the field. I lie on the floor in front of him, thinking how weird it is that he was always so fat, and now he looks like he's starving to death.

"Do you ever think about God," I ask him.

"Nope."

The word slips quickly out of his mouth. He doesn't look up.

"Never?"

"I don't think he would even know my name, Lee. He'd say 'Bob who?'"

"But don't you think there might be something . . ."

I stop and study my dad's face. He appears half amused, half befuddled, and capable of being annoyed in a nano-second.

"I suppose so, Lee, but . . ."

"Clearly there has to be something," I insist. I pull my legs up to get up off the floor so I can sit closer to him.

"The earth revolves around the sun. Flowers grow. Wind blows. It's pretty spectacular."

"Yes." He moves his shoulders, does that bony slipping thing, and I know I should stop, but I don't.

"Do you ever pray?"

"Nope!" Another quick slither of bony shoulders. I am treading in very dangerous waters.

"I do."

"Really?"

"Yep."

He purses his lips and studies me.

"I ask for help."

"How 'bout that."

"You have to admit that life is uncanny . . . you know, there is a way things work out? Coincidences?"

"I suppose."

"I guess that's all I'm saying. I don't know what the fuck it is, Dad. But it's something."

"Your language is awful; you take after your mother."

He looks at me a moment, smiles mischievously and then returns to his reading.

I move around behind him and slither my fingers through his hair, pulling it up into a dip on top of his head.

"Hey, Dad, maybe it's time to change your hair."

"Why?"

"Why not? A life crisis, cancer. It's an opportunity to change your hair. You know, live life with reckless abandon. Change your hair?"

"I don't know," he says, smoothing his hair out with his hand as if it will be taken away. "I've had this haircut ever since I was a boy."

∽

It is morning, and we drive into Brookline to get a baseline CAT scan of my father's lungs. On the way, we chat, my father telling stories about the business he built. He loves to tell these stories now, all about these people in California, these people in Connecticut, and all the ways he maneuvered difficult personalities, moving big deals, selling doohickeys for the aerospace industry. He is very proud of his accomplishments, and as I sit and listen, watching him smile and move his shoulders and laugh, *Ha!* and *Humph! humph! You shoulda seen'em,* he squeals with delight. He's never seen anything like it. *Ha! Humph! Humph!*

He also wants to hear about Tom's new entrepreneurial ventures. The latest is he has joined forces with an old friend in Oregon to resuscitate a failing telecom company. And Dad especially loves to hear about our garden plans. *Too many trees, Lee. No room to grow.*

When Dad first met Tom, almost two decades before, Tom was always on his way to exotic locales—Japan, Africa, France—and all Dad could say was this: *I like Tommy but I think he could use a new compass.*

We laughed, but his message was clear. A sense of duty and responsibility was not Tom's strong suit, and it so clearly had been my father's philosophy and prison. Not too long afterward, I followed Tom to France, where we lived for a little more than a year. I knew my father was unhappy about my departure. I was leaving a good job doing research at Tufts Medical School in the Department of Psychiatry for the distant possibility of a job at an English language magazine in Paris called *Passion*.

"What the hell is in France," he asked. "It's just a bunch of French people."

A week before I left, we walked around the garden together looking at the tomatoes, zinnias, and dahlias as he struggled for something to say. "Well, Lee," he finally croaked. "You seem to have a sense of adventure. I never did. Now, I wish I had."

Back in Cambridge a few years later, Tom and I drove out to Framingham to tell Mom and Dad that we were going to get married. Dad and I snuck out to the back deck to smoke and chat.

"What did you do," he asked laughing. "Beat him over the head with a hammer?"

"I beg your pardon, Father, dear. He begged me. He begged me."

"*Ha!*" Pops laughed. "*Ha!* Somehow, knowing Tommy, I doubt that." I bopped him one in the shoulder, a quick pound from the back of my hand. He wiggled away and laughed more heartily.

Pop is quiet on the morning we drive into Boston for his first chemotherapy appointment. He lies back in the seat with his eyes closed and I prompt him on questions he needs to ask the doctor. He talks about wanting a physical therapist, and I know he wants to get better and is, for the moment, believing he will. I push aside all other knowledge and climb into that boat with him, believing in the possibility, believing in the miracle of medicine.

He is so weak now. We get to the center and park, and he motions for a wheelchair, and when we crowd into the elevator, I watch him move his head from one side to the other, studying our traveling companions unabashedly as the others smile uncomfortably and study him, too, everyone trying to gauge the severity of one another's illness, the likelihood of death, and if death seems likely, how soon, and if it seems unlikely, then how come?

"Hello, Mr. Montgomery," the oncologist's assistant trumpets. She is a little spit of a woman, maybe twenty, a smiling face with long, curly hair, a dark complexion, her eyes perfect circles the color of chestnuts. Her name is Rosanne and my father is in love with her.

"How are you today," she yells.

"Lousy," he yells back. He laughs. "We're late." He looks strange sitting in the wheelchair in front of this tall reception desk. Rosanne has to get up on her tiptoes to see him on the other side.

"No big deal," she says with a wave of her hand. She hands over a few pieces of paper and directs him to the waiting room on the other side of the elevator to get his blood tested.

"Then the doctor will see you and I'll take you down to the tenth floor to get your chemo."

Dana-Farber's chemotherapy unit is busy, busy on Wednesdays. Bright lights and crowds of people with wigs and pretty scarves wrapped around their bald heads pack the waiting rooms, which are full of snacks and drinks. Later, when we enter the unit itself, a large room with different stations, we see assorted people sitting around with tubes hooked into their veins. They sit in easy chairs with personal televisions hooked into walls next to oxygen and IV pumps. As we walk the corridors of the chemo unit, I feel like we have stepped inside a dream. It's otherworldly. Windows line each of the four treatment areas, which surround the nurses' station. The sheer number of people sitting here hooked into bags of chemicals, reading books, eating, and watching their favorite TV shows is astounding. Few look sick enough to die; rather, they look like the bald products of some super clone experiment: the new millennium human.

This first day of chemo is light and lovely. As we sit in one waiting room after another with other cancer patients, everyone smiles, hopeful, courteous, and patient.

When we see the doctor, Dad asks all of his questions, and I check them off the list.

"I just want to be feeling better," he says.

"Well, you should be feeling better," the doctor says.

I study the doctor and feel as though a chicken bone is caught in my throat. *You should be feeling better? You're dying, but you should be feeling better? In the meantime? Soon? After all?*

My father says things that make it clear that he truly believes he will be feeling better, that he is simply ignoring the paragraphs that read *there is no cure for your disease at this point,* ignoring the fact that he is a guinea pig here, and that they are saying to him, *If this chemo doesn't help you, it may help someone else down the line.*

He is told that there may be some nausea and other side effects in the first forty-eight hours.

We ask about others in the trial.

The doctor reels off some numbers and mentions three patients who went off the study because of side effects: One had numb fingers, another had heart disease. And the other guy? The doctor doesn't say.

When the doctor leaves, my father, lying on an examining table, turns to me.

"I wanted to ask about the other guy," he says, "but I was too afraid." Daddy-o, Mr. Bones, looks so small there stretched out on the table.

"Me, too, Daddy-o," I say. "Me, too."

My father eats all day as the chemo drips into his veins. The nurses rush in and out with bags, first of fluids, then of cisplatin, then adriamycin. Before we leave that night, fluorouracil (5-FU) is loaded into the portable pump. It is the size of a transistor radio and is attached to the system of catheters placed inside my father's shoulder. It hums for twenty-four hours a day, and every once in a while makes a weird grinding, whining moan. They give Dad a little sack for the pump so he can carry it over his shoulder like a purse.

We are given a long list of instructions about the pump: who to call, when to call. Codes to punch in. Flashes and beep sounds. At first, I hated the pump but soon grew to believe it was our only hope. Over the next two months, I found I would do anything to keep that pump going. As long as it was attached, there was more time.

Because Dad eats all day at chemo, I am unbearably happy. He eats half of a bran muffin and fruit salad. A half sandwich and a bag of potato chips. He eats a cookie. Female nurses, social workers, and nutritionists file in and out all day long and I see my father buoyed by all the attention. He eats more.

Everything said or implicated is engineered toward hope. By the time we climb into the car after eight hours of bright lights and IV pumps and cute nurses, armed with prescriptions to protect against fungus and infections and nausea and constipation and pain, we are high on the stuff. We are high on the possibility of life. Chemotherapy is a gas.

Daddy-o talks all the way home, reviewing the day, what the nurses said or didn't say. *She is a pistol!* He laughs about the head nurse in his charge. *She is efficient!* He laughs again. *She works hard!* He laughs again. Behind him, the lights of the highway hang in a cool late winter dusk, framed by the car windows, and I see that he is smiling.

He tells me a family story I didn't remember or hadn't heard before, about how Uncle Albert, his mother's brother, was disowned by the family because he walked out on his wife. He was a trumpet player and he had a son named Richard, a nice fella, Dad says, who married a bleached blonde.

"Oh, she was something," Dad hoots, his shoulders and knees squished together in a happy bunch.

"Loud and vulgar," he laughs again, this time accompanied with a full *humph!* "She was great."

"You like your women that way, don't you, Dad?"

"Hmm? How's that?"

"You like your women blonde, loud, and vulgar!"

"Ha! I suppose," he laughs again. "Boy, was she a pistol! Ha!"

*   *   *

When we arrive home, Dad sits in his easy chair telling stories about the hospital. Mother lies in bed listening and across the room from Dad in the other chair sits Stoyan's father, Kiral, an orthopedic surgeon from Bulgaria who came to work for my parents years ago as a companion for mother and has since become their great friend. Kiral calls my father *Bub* and for reasons I have never really understood, Dad calls Kiral the Holy Spirit or, as Kiral says, *the Oly Spirt*.

Because Kiral cannot practice medicine in the United States without many more years in school, he decided to study to become a physical therapist in Amsterdam. When he left the United States, his son, Stoyan, took over his job with my mother. Even far away, the Holy Spirit remained important. Both Mom and Dad have read Kiral's letters to me over the phone and laughed hysterically at all of his extremely dirty jokes. When my father was first diagnosed with cancer and we all reeled with the news, the Holy Spirit did what no one else could. He called from Europe and peppered his usual fare of dirty jokes with cancer jokes, pushing my father into riotous laughter.

The fact that my parents come to find themselves surrounded by Bulgarians, whom my mother calls Vulgarians, is another one of my life's great unanswered questions. They make Dad laugh and teach Mother to love watching soccer, how to say *Let's make love* in Bulgarian, and how to play grabby-ass in the pool. "Grabby-ass" is Dad's term.

"Where's Mum?"

"She's playing grabby-ass in the pool."

"Gabby-ass?"

"That, too."

Everyone has nicknames. The Kid or Sweet Stuff, *Oly Spirt,* Bub. And Mom?

"Toots," Stoyan calls her. "C'mon, Toots, move your ass." He chases her through the house, her limping like the real McCoy, pushing her buggy. He carries her drink, and when she farts, he shouts, "Middle C, F sharp, Whoa, Nelly! Jesus, the whole rhythm section."

The Bulgarians are part of the family, such as it is. They are fabulous cooks, wonderful friends, and great entertainers. They smell of garlic and onions and eat strange and hearty things: porridges from the Black Forest, soups of root vegetables, and whole milk yogurt with torn pieces of pumpernickel bread.

Some days, when Mumzy is slightly numb from drinking more gin than would seem humanly possible, she appears to be falling in love over and over again with *Oly Spirt* or The Kid. As it happens, the *Oly Spirt* has counseled mother on matters of love, and love making—particularly, my mother admits one day sheepishly, "going down on your father."

"Jesus, Mother," I say. We are walking around the shallow end of the pool.

The *Oly Spirt* mentions something about balls, Mother tells me, "But I don't do balls," she says. "Never have, never will. That means, not with your father's or any other: No tennis. No golf. No pool."

Later that night, after his first round of chemo, we put Pops to bed where he stays for a few days, nauseous but okay. I wash his face with a washcloth, prepare meals, and lie with him in the late afternoons, hassling him to get up to gargle, hassling him to drink more water. On the third day, we awake to a late spring snow and my father insists on going to the bank. I watch him struggle into his jeans, grabbing the pump to sling over his shoulder, looking like death itself. We wander to the car. I'm careful to hold onto him, a gesture he doesn't much appreciate.

"Wait, Dad, let me . . ."

He opens the door himself and climbs in. When we get to the bank, I try to help him out of the car and inside the building, and again he refuses, struggling on his own. I follow him and watch the faces of the tellers as they greet him, faces of women who've known him for many years and who see him as a tired and thin old man. We all stand expressionless, trying not to register the changes we see, and I watch my father look at all of us, knowing exactly what we're thinking, but not saying a word.

Soon we are back in Boston to visit the surgeon. A section of the incision from his surgery that hasn't healed is draining a green liquid, has been for months. Initially, the incision contained a stitch that did not dissolve and was removed a month or so after surgery. Now Smiling Bob, in his surgeon clothes, the legs of his scrubs clinging to his black socks, to reveal his weird long feet, tells us the wound is caused by a tumor.

"I don't know about him," I say to Dad as we get into the elevator.

"Me neither," Dad says.

When the door opens into the enormous hallway of the hospital, I wheel my father around in circles very fast.

"Live a little," I say. "God, Smiling Bob . . . cheery ain't he?"

"Why bother," Dad says, referring to my criticism. "Why

the hell bother. It doesn't do a bit of good, Lee, not one bit of good."

I stop and study Pop for a minute. He gives me a sad smile.

"Got the parking ticket?"

"Uh-oh," I say, rummaging through my purse.

"Oh no," Dad says. "You didn't."

"I didn't. I didn't." I hold the ticket up for him. "I didn't! Ha!"

When we get home, I lie with him. In a few days, it will be time for me to head home. He turns, rolls over. His chemo pump whines. His eyes are closed. I watch him and begin to silently recite the names of all the flowers he has planted in his life, the rows of dahlias, zinnias, portulaca, strawflowers, asters, blue blazers, pink magics, cornflowers, red fox, and blue boys. Each year he traces out plans for his gardens. When the sun gets warm and the days get longer, he wanders around the garden pulling up the mulch from the fall. There is the smell of the earth beneath the damp rotting leaves. He digs with his hand, cupping a handful of soil, squeezing it into a ball then flicking a finger into the soil ball a couple of times. If it remains intact or falls away in heavy clumps, it's too wet to work. March is generally too early, but there have been years. It's possible. His hands reach into the air as he sleeps. I wonder if he dreams of the earth crumbling in his hands like chocolate cake. Dry enough to get started, ready to till. It seems to me now that there is nothing as beautiful as hands in the earth, planting flowers. It's an act of faith. Planting flowers implies the gardener believes he will live long enough to see their blooms.

12

ESCAPES

May 1999
Portland, Oregon

I am back in Oregon when my father receives the news that his tumors are shrinking. The doctors talk about a tumor on his liver that we had only previously heard about in passing from the surgeon. This tumor raises various questions for Bob, Lael, and me, questions that escalate and, in the end, result in yet another call to The Oncologist. It's at this moment that we finally learn the true extent of my father's disease.

"Do you want to know or don't you," Lael asks me over the phone after she speaks to The Oncologist.

"I don't know," I say.

"Do you or don't you?"

"Yes. Okay."

I sit down and get a notepad.

Tumors here. Tumors there. Tumors everywhere.

I write them all down, and then draw them carefully, using the dimensions in centimeters to create tumors the size of pencil boxes, bigger and smaller, careful with my measurements. Stomach: a tumor the size of a baseball; rib: a tumor the size and shape of a cigarette; liver: a flat one that was the size of a small notebook, now a candy bar; kidneys: one bigger than a nickel. And the fluid in his heart? I don't know what it looks like, but any image I can conjure is evil and dreary.

I lie on the floor of my office after I get this news. I can see pieces of sky through the window. And I imagine floating out the window and all around the rooftops, through the cloudy town, assembling strength, gathering and categorizing my father, trying to organize four decades of memory into an afternoon.

One of the categories is the gifts that he gave me. Often they were tools of escape: a small shovel to dig out of snowdrifts; a clanking, folding ladder to hang from the window in order to flee fire. Pop gives me instructions on how to use the tools and where to store them. The shovel was to go in my car trunk. The ladder, made of metal bars and chain link, was to pile under my bed.

Pop was so proud to offer these things, but at the time, I was mystified. The shovel was a present he actually wrapped and placed by the fireplace to feign the Santa thing even though I was twenty-four. That Christmas morning, I looked at the shovel, then back at him. "A shovel?" I asked confused. "A shovel?"

At the time, I did not know that these gifts would come to seem sacred to me. In fact, I don't begin to understand it fully until hearing the worst from Lael, and I realize what they say about life is true. It does end, and now all those years of living far apart seem so tragic.

Somehow now, watching the sky turn darker still, I understand for the first time that this is not a game we can win. I take to my bed for days, staring at the ceiling, heavy with this knowledge. I fall into darkness, imagining my father dying, and then when I become unable to process this possibility, I manufacture hope again; just a glimpse of it. I know it's the end, but I also absolutely refuse to accept it—if we could only do this or that, if he could only get stronger, if we could only find some obscure treatment.

"I understand you think that I am terminal," Pop tells Lael. "Your mother tells me you think I'm terminal."

"Can you fucking believe that?" Lael says. "I tell Mother to shape up, sober up, stop whining, because he is not getting any better, and then she tells him that I think he is dying!"

"As if it's your fault!" I say.

"'I understand you think I'm terminal!'"

A few days before I next head back East, Pop telephones me to help me arrange for the shuttle service that never comes. It has been many months since he has reached for the telephone of his own volition. He is not a man who ever calls to chat. He calls only to relay information.

"Hi, Pops."

"Hello there, I wanted to give you the phone numbers for the limousine."

As he reads them off, I imagine him taking the time to think of it. Lying there with, perhaps, *Road and Track* open on his chest and thinking about how I might make my way from the airport to Framingham. I see him pulling himself out of bed to find a telephone book and hunting through the listings, running one of his short fingers down the names, writing the numbers down, and picking up the phone.

Traditionally May is a triumphant regenerative time, a time of planting, May flowers, May baskets, and May poles, but on this trip to Boston, initially slated to be a week, it is another round of chemotherapy for Pop.

I arrive at midnight to find Mom and Pop, sound asleep and smaller than before. I wake them up, kiss them hello in the darkness and tell them about my trip—canceled flights, cars that never showed up.

"But hey, folks," I say. "You would not believe it. It's seventy degrees in Chicago!"

I touch my father's arms and they are only bones.

It soon becomes clear that there is something wrong with my eyes—they are weepy and sick. The night before I'm to drive Dad to chemotherapy, I lie awake nursing a phenomenal pain in my head. I want to go downstairs and get help but know there's no strength left in those rooms. It's a sad, startling realization. In the morning, I get up at dawn and go to the emergency room at the Framingham Hospital where I sit and eventually get antibiotics and eye ointments and drops. I have pinkeye so I cannot touch my father. My eyes are swollen and runny and I look like a goon.

When I return from the hospital, I make breakfast—Pop a piece of toasting white and an egg; me, coffee and cigarettes, as many as I can muster; and Mom, a gin minty.

I make it my mission to cook. I make beef and pork

roasts; tomato, basil, and mozzarella salads; my father's favorite pasta, which Susan introduced us to. I call her at the office for the recipe, interrupting a meeting, and though she is insanely busy as a corporate attorney, she halts everything to spell out how to sear the scallops just so and how to sauté the cream sauce, the shrimp, and green onions for BD.

In less than two weeks, after the chemo, Dad will undergo another CAT scan to restage the cancer and we will all turn down the last bend in the road: the beginning of in and out of hospitals, ambulances, cars. The beginning of the end. Though we all hold hope carefully in our hands like water we see our father growing smaller and smaller as he silently slips into himself.

The morning after my arrival, I look out our windows and see that spring is here in earnest. The daffodils and crocus reach out, the asparagus is making a show. In the back field, the daisies are almost waist high and though he is weak, my father is full of stories of farms, his carpenter grandfather, business missions and associates. We lie in his bed as he tells me stories, laughing, recollecting, and slipping his bony shoulders up and down. In turn, I read him stories from a book sent by my sister called *Choices in Healing.* It is a book my father never opens, so I read him the stories of people who survive nasty stomach cancers.

"See?" I say. "Dad, see?"

"Yeah, yeah, yeah," he says, closing his eyes.

He is very tired, and very weak.

To make matters worse, the morphine patches that he began applying the week before to ease the pain in his stomach are making him sick so he now has dry heaves, too.

"This is new," he announces at breakfast in between gagging, slamming his hand against the table.

"Damn it."

He struggles up and walks on his stick legs back to bed.

When we go to chemo, he lies in his own room. The nurse and he are good friends now, sharing stories of families, gardening, and built-in pools. Dad has told her everything there is to know about engineering a built-in pool, and she can barely contain her excitement. She has children Dad calls the "little Indians." She comes in and out carrying bags of fluids and poisons, hooking them in and hanging them on the metal hanger, checking the infusion pump numbers. Dad stretches out and I sit at the foot of his bed in a metal chair. In between her visits, Dad and I read and chat about everything and nothing at all.

Earlier that morning when we meet with The Oncologist, I urge him to talk to Dad about other tactics—visualization and relaxation—and The Oncologist courteously tells me to leave my father alone.

"If it occurs to your father as a good thing, then it would be, but since it hasn't . . ." He smiles.

I look at my father, who is sticking his tongue out at me.

"All right then," I raise my hands in a full-scale surrender. "I'll shut up."

But a million arguments sound in my head. How could anyone possibly believe that? After all, had chemotheraphy suddenly occurred to my father as a good thing?

"Sometimes it doesn't matter what you do, Lee," my father tells me. He lies in his hospital bed. "Do you know what I'm talking about? It just doesn't matter. Sometimes there's nothing you can do."

He smiles and I understand he is telling me something that I do not want to believe.

I am silent, overwhelmed. I wash my hands and sit on his bed and play with his fingers and we look out the window together, a window that overlooks smoking hospital towers against a low New England sky.

My father refuses to eat all day long, so I eat everything—sandwiches, potato chips, and cookies. By the end of the day, my stomach is full. I feel like I'm going to throw up.

We drive home in silence. Dad is spread out, feeling awful. When we put him to bed, he slips away for days, rallying only for a little while to argue about the whiskey barrels we will purchase in lieu of a garden this year. It is my assignment to purchase the whiskey barrels, and my father tells me there are three places we can go and that I need to call to get prices. When I deliver the information to his bedside, providing measurements and prices, he says, "You should probably go to Diehls."

"But that's in Wellesley and they are only five dollars cheaper than Russell's two miles down the road."

"I know it," he says.

"I'll spend that in gas."

He purses his lips and smiles.

"Not quite," he says.

"The question is, Dad, do they have the good barrels?"

"How the hell would I know."

"Well, you're the expert."

"I know it," he says closing his eyes. "Don't forget the dirt, part compost, part potting soil."

I am nervous about my assignment, wanting these whiskey barrels to be the best, and when I get there and see that they're not, I call home. He instructs me to get them anyway and, though I am unhappy with the barrel, for once I do as I'm told. When he finally gets up a few days later to go to the bank with The Kid, he inspects the barrels on his way in from the car and says, "What the hell were you bitching about? They are fine. They are just fine."

"But they're not the right ones, the old ones."

"I know it," he says, "but who gives a shit, Lee. They work."

Later, when my father naps, I walk through the field of daisies, a field my father is proud of now, but which during the old days was the subject of many arguments. I wanted to keep the daisies; he wanted the field mowed. Now, he is proud that the daisies are so bountiful and so high.

As I walk along the fence, I remember the days when it was just wire with pieces of torn sheet to warn the horses of its presence, but over the years, my father has built post-and-rail all the way down to the bottom of the property. I find a corner that has shorter rails to accommodate a shorter than standard span. It must have taken him a weekend at least to work it out, sawing off the rails he'd found in an old woodpile and saved for years, just in case a project like this arose.

At the end of the field, I slip through the fence onto a grassy lane that leads to our neighbor's pond. The lane has become overgrown. The grass is tall and old trees have fallen in the path. For many years, this lane was fastidiously tended. Old Mr. Fitts mowed it every week, making an elegant grassy carriage trail that wound down and around to a pond where I spent many afternoons as a child, skating in the winter, pollywogging in the spring. As a teenager, I blew butts and boys and drank Boone's Farm apple wine on a moss patch not far from the pond. Though I always approached the pond on the carriage path, I got home by following the streams' paths, drifting, walking their bottoms, water up to my knees, picking cattails and pussy willows, until I saw the field and, beyond that, home. I do this now after sitting and watching the pollywogs in the murky water.

I know few things in life as well as these streams, even though they too change with time. Some have completely disappeared, but the main ones remain the same, and I follow their trails, wading up to my knees, without bothering to remove my sneakers or roll up my jeans, making my way through the woods. Back in the field, I look for remnants of my brother's tree house in the old elm and find the wooden boards of the well. They are so rotten, they disintegrate in my hand as I pull them up to see the clear water below.

In these final months, it is during my endless walking around this area that I begin to understand what saved me. There was magic and comfort in this landscape and in the kindness of the people who surrounded me. True, I spent many afternoons sitting at the dining room table with Mother while she talked on the phone, or cried about the dead babies, but it is also true that at some point it occured to me to walk out the door and wander up and down the streets. I began to stop at various houses, making friends. Mr. and Mrs. Fitts lived next door; their children were all grown up and gone. I would arrive and play in the milk room of their barn, and then knock on the door where Mrs. Fitts would receive me. I'd sit at her kitchen table and we'd talk and she'd give me cookies, and then I would move along, usually to the Wellingtons', where I had three friends: Mrs. Wellington and her two daughters, Mimi and Barbie. Sometimes I stayed for hours. For a few years I was there almost all the time.

On a corner down the road was a long winding driveway that led to a huge stone house full of Gray Nuns, an order of Episcopal nuns. When I was eight, the nuns and their stone house came to have great appeal. The boss, Mother Stell, dropped by every once in a while to try to save my mother's soul, and they had become friendly, so I knew I would be welcome. The first time I ventured down the driveway, and up onto the front porch, I wanted to ask about God. I hadn't yet knocked and a large wooden door opened and a nun, three times my size, stood dressed all in gray, wearing the weirdest hat. It looked like she had wings on her head. Her skin was pale like dough and she wore the smallest rimless glasses. She looked down at me.

"Well hello," she said.

I nodded.

"Well, hello. May I help you?" Behind her was a painting of God. He looked like I imagined God would: flowing white robes in a cloud with a long white beard.

"I'm here to see God," I said. Mother Stell smiled and took my hand and led me to a small chapel where she instructed me to sit and wait. I sat and stared at the candles on the altar and saw a white buzzing light rise and fall. It buzzed and buzzed. I sat for a long time watching the light flicker around, wondering if somewhere on the other side of the wall there was a nun with a flashlight. When the little nun, Sister Annie, came to get me, I told her I thought I saw something.

"What's he look like?" she asked.

"A little white light is all."

I told no one else, thinking that if I did, it would be taken away. But once that was settled, I wanted to know what it was like to have the inside line to the other side. I wanted to see the inside of a nun's closet. I wanted to eat what the nuns ate. I wanted to know if like doctors' wives, nuns cut the crusts off of sandwiches. (They didn't.) So I visited often, doing these things: seeing God, looking into closets, holding Sister Annie's tiny hands, playing cards, eating tuna sandwiches.

I made friends with neighbors in every direction: There was the old lady across the street who lived in a house her grandfather had built. In the other direction was another old lady who, I'd heard, had dead people buried in her yard. Further down Winch Street there was a house that was three hundred years old, owned by a pretty woman named Louise who was a good friend of my mother's. Her house had very low ceilings, a fireplace as wide as the living room, and a bookshelf that doubled as a staircase, allowing settlers to escape and hide from Indian attackers. Almost every day I had adventures and then on my way home I stopped at the florist, who let me dig through the dead flower pile to find the pretty ones. Did I bring them to the nuns? To the ladies? To Mother? I can't remember.

∞

Later that afternoon, as I make my way through the field, I study the back of the house, thinking that my father has spent most of his weekends looking at the same tableau.

Today, the daisies and lilacs behind the house are in full
bloom, the forsythia has already come and gone. I eventually find myself downstairs in the barn, in my father's workshop, rooting around, smelling the musty basement smell
mixed with pony and manure. In the corner is a Windsor
chair my father had told me he had tried to work on around
Christmas but didn't finish. I examine the chair, trying to
figure out what he wasn't able to do when I hear the pony
next door whinny. I peek into her stall to look at her. She
is almost identical to Happy Birthday: dapples and a white
mane and tail. She's always been aloof, but today she is talk-
ative, nickering incessantly. I leave my father's workshop,
grab a brush and walk into her stall, and when I stretch out
my palm, she nibbles and licks the salt from my skin. I move
the brush gently down her coat, and stuff my nose into her
neck, remembering the smell of Happy as a child, brushing,
smoothing, and pulling out tangles in her mane—and then
I begin to wander all through the barn, up and down the
stairs, picking through junk, smelling the barn smells of hay
and grains, rodents, horse manure, and the sharpness of
horses.

Built in the mid 1800s, it was originally a dairy barn with
two proper floors for animals and an attic for hay. The main
floor had been built to store machinery, and there was a
basement of large rooms with earthen floors accessible by
a wooden ramp. My parents used the attic to store junk;
antiques, milk cans, egg carton boxes made of wood. The
ground floor was the home of Mother's grain experiments;
my grandmother Montgomery's electric band saw on which,
most Saturdays, she cut long newspaper faggots she soaked
in chemicals and made "fireplace rainbows" to sell in local

country stores; a large stack of firewood; and a two-car garage. Downstairs in the basement was the horse stable.

In the old days, the barn's rotting walls were riddled with pinholes that let in fine, magical beams of sunlight. One summer morning, when I was about thirteen, I was in the barn during a partial solar eclipse, and tiny crescent moons were projected everywhere I looked. Bob was there working on an MG TD that he and Dad had built together. It was hot. I had been hanging around watching him, hoping he'd ask me to hand him a wrench or something, when he stood up and his face was covered by crescent moons. He told me to run into the house and grab a marker and a few of Dad's T-shirts. He had me put them on one after another and then, standing me in a spot thick with miniature images of the eclipse, traced inky moons on each one.

∞

When I return to the house, I run into my mother, who teeters a bit from too much gin.

"He's leaving," she tells me.

"What do you mean," I ask her.

"What I said. He's on his way."

I look at her and am silent.

"He's dying," she screams. "Your father is dying."

Hope is a funny business. My mother and father do not ask the doctor questions, but Lael, Bob, and I do. We know the extent of his disease—even if we hope we can change it. Every step of the way, we make telephone calls to doctors and scour the Internet, but Mom and Dad don't seem to want to know, or perhaps they've made the assumption that the doctor will tell them everything, which the doctor does not.

Mother continues to stay home when we go to the doctor. The trip is too difficult in the wheelchair, she tells us. But I believe that the trip is too difficult for other reasons, and this becomes the game: the game of hope. The less known, the better. The less she sees the scales tipping toward the inevitable, the easier we all carry on. Still, the truth leaks into our hearts slowly but surely as we see Dad grow smaller and smaller. We pretend for as long as we can. We pretend that it's not happening, and the doctors let us.

A few days after Dad's chemotherapy, a dear friend of his, a business buddy, comes over, and they talk for hours. Dad is all jazzed up, happy. I hear him hooting in the other room, having a ball. Later, we get up and go to the bank, and he seems stronger than he has for a while, but that night, he sinks deeply. He throws up all night and in the morning runs a fever; his blood pressure is very low. After a few calls to the doctor, I bundle him up and take him to the emergency room, where we wait for four hours to get him admitted. All afternoon I circle back and forth from his little ER room to the phone, where I call Mother, Lael, and Bob one right after another to give updates.

The following night, through the small window of an ambulance, Pop waves, now a small old man, bound up in white blankets, holding a vase of lilacs on his lap. He's being transferred to the hospital in Boston. He gives me his wallet for safekeeping and when I return home, I sit on the bed and take it apart, itemizing everything: driver's license, bright eyes and half smile in the photo, expiring on his birthday in 1999;

Master Card, LL Bean and Exxon cards; Framingham Public Library, Star Market Value Rewards, and Social Security cards.

I place them all with the other things that I've been collecting, as if these objects can testify to the truth: Hospital bracelets, garden diagrams, plans for cellar doors, and a one-and-a-half-inch bore. I memorize my father's license and Social Security number and itemize the contents of his wallet. In my personal journal under the date of November 23, 1998, I see his name handwritten on a small piece of paper with *Brigham and Women's Hospital* printed at the top. Filled in the allotted lined spaces is the number of his first hospital room after the surgery.

In the morning, I find him in a shiny, hopeful Dana-Farber wing for cancer patients. Dad has his own hermetically sealed room. There are several doors leading into the wing—one door must be closed in order to open the other. Some patients wear masks, and every one has his or her own nurse. After talking to the nurse and learning nothing except that they've tripled his pain medicine, I find my father snoozing in a sunny room. When he awakes later, I am sitting in a chair next to his bed reading *People Magazine*. He smiles.

"Hi," I say. "I filled the barrels."

"You did," he says.

"Yep, well, not really. Not the flowers. I put soil in them. Mother's talking about getting the flowers at Russell's."

"Did you drill holes and put screens in the bottom?"

"No, was I supposed to?"

"Yes."

He purses his lips, shakes his head.

"Lee, you are cursed by your ancestors."

I laugh.

"What do you mean?"

"No patience."

"Shit," I say. "I can't believe I did that."

He sits there half smiling, stoned out of his gourd on morphine, but remains sharp as a tack, sharp enough to laugh as he relays my blunder to Bob and Susan when they visit later that night.

∞

With more morphine, Dad now needs a walker because the drug makes him too stoned.

"I gotta get up," he says.

I give him a hand. He stands, a little shaky, with both hands on the walker.

"How do you like my buggy?"

"It's great."

I then watch him pick it up and walk to the bathroom.

"Dad?"

"What?" He turns and looks at me over his shoulder.

"You're not supposed to carry it. It's supposed to carry you. That's the point."

"Huh, what do you know?" he says as he closes the door.

A minute later, he appears at the door, holding the walker off the ground.

"Dad." I stand and walk toward him. You need to put this on the ground and have it help you walk."

"Yeah?"

"Yeah."

He puts it down.

"Now lean on it. Do you see how it can help keep your balance?"

"Yeah. Yeah. Yeah," he says impatiently pointing it toward me. "You're in my way."

I step out of the way and watch him lift the walker and walk back to bed.

When my father's eyes close for a nap, I move out into the hallway to see if I can track down some information. My questions swirl here, and I cannot find any answers. I call the oncologist several times, but he does not return my call. The nurse tells me that my father does not have pneumonia and that the blood counts that indicated an infection at the Framingham hospital were not accurate.

"We'll take him off the 5-FU pump tomorrow," she continues.

"What?" I say. "What do you mean take him off the pump?"

She checks the file. "It says here to take him off the pump." At that minute the social worker arrives and as we stand in front of the nurses' station, I begin to cry.

"Does he know that?" I ask.

"I don't know," she says.

"Why are you taking him off the pump?" I ask.

"You have to talk to the doctor," she says.

"I cannot reach the doctor," I say. "I have called three times and he has not yet returned the call."

The social worker takes me to a small room where I cry for an hour and when we surface again a nurse tells me the doctor is on his way. A few minutes later, I find him standing behind the nurses' station. As I ask him questions, he flips through the file to find the answers.

The nurse is wrong. The pump stays on, and I am relieved. There will be a visiting infusion nurse who will administer fluids every day to keep Pop from dehydrating. Arranging that involves a bit of rigmarole. Logistics. Telephone calls. Money transactions for the fluid company. And so forth.

A little later, I return to my father and watch him sleep in a late afternoon spring sun. Tomorrow, after the pump is filled, we will go home. When I tell him that, he turns, smiles sleepily, and says, "Oh, goody."

∞

Leaving the Dana-Farber wing is complicated. We wait for doctors to give discharge instructions. We wait for nurses to contradict the doctors' instructions. It is hours before we are given the go-ahead and by then we're confused. Even so, we are so relieved to get the hell out of there that we grab the long list of discharge medicines, the handful of new prescriptions, and spin down the halls with Dad in a wheelchair to find the car and make our way west. Dad is ecstatic about going home and, stoned on morphine and free of pain, is more playful than he has been on past rides. He wants me to take the back roads to avoid the traffic. I smile at him. This is Daddy-o, sick as hell, but at the top of his game, The King of Back Roads. We turn off the highway and, ready for adventure, follow the Sudbury River. Dad rolls down his window, lets the wind blow in what's left of his hair, and shouts instructions as we bend around the river. I am completely lost, but he keeps shouting left, right, often after we have sailed triumphantly by the turn.

"Give me one of those cigarettes," he says.

As far as I know, he hasn't smoked since his surgery.

"No, I don't think that's such a good idea."

"C'mon," he urges.

"You sure?"

"Yes." He holds out his hand. I fumble in my purse and hand him one, which he lights, and begins to cough and cough and cough. He throws it out.

"God, that tastes awful."

My father is firmly seated in the passenger seat: my father, the old man.

"Hey, you know, the seat belt is not working," I say.

"Really?" he says. He leans over and gives it a tug. "We'll take it back to Buick and say, 'Hey, you know what, the fucking seat belts aren't working.'"

He laughs and then launches into a story about a trick he played on his partner and boss. The story involves widgets and a Japanese salesman, and it is long and complicated, and I cannot quite follow it, but it ends with Dad walking into his partner's office and saying something about the Motherfucking Japanese that he thinks is very funny (he was stationed in the South Pacific during World War II). He is so stoned he laughs and laughs and laughs. I laugh because he's laughing so we miss all of our turns and get completely lost, but it doesn't matter because we are having the time of our lives.

When we arrive home, the bedroom feels like a tomb. It is silent and the air feels full of cotton. Mother sits with her back to us, turns uselessly, her eyes seared into a drunken stare. Her words are muffled; she can barely speak.

"Now, who is it that you would like me to invite to your funeral," she asks.

Later, Mother careens around the corner with her buggy and takes a tumble in the hallway. She is wildly bombed. Her eyes cannot focus, and she begins to crawl, shouting incoherently. Pop climbs out of bed and we go to her.

"Don't touch me," she yells.

"For Christ's sakes, Barbara."

She swings at us, reacting to a drama we are not part of. Dad and I exchange sad, worried glances and move away. Neither of us is strong enough to pick her up on our own so she must spend the night on the floor. She crawls around the bed, mumbling. As I watch her, I feel an aching in my chest spread to my hands and legs, a restlessness that urges me to run! And in my mind, I do. I run everywhere: through all the rooms, through towns, through years, finally stopping in a year when the kitchen is yellow, a year that I am old enough to drive. In the corner of the frame, a hand reaches for me. An ironing board crashes, the iron splays steam and water across the linoleum, and there she is spread out on the floor.

Mother. Drunk and spewing insults.

I remember so little about Mother during high school, but suddenly this memory floats clearly before me. I watch myself kneel and place my hands around my mother's neck, pushing my thumbs together. I tighten my hands until the words stop. She doesn't appear frightened, though her hands reach for mine to loosen the grip, and there we sit breathless, frozen in time, and I study her sad, sad face, her eyes bluer than steel. My brain stops. I can feel the rage, and the terror of finding myself with my hands around my mother's neck. I let go of her then and run out of the house.

Now what? It has taken so many years to reconstruct that scene, and now that I have and it floats before me so brilliantly clear, striking, and pathetic, I can only examine it from a distance as if it is made of fire. I feel burning shame and sadness, rage and what? *What do I do with all of this?*

I turn back to the present to find Pop lying in bed; Mother is still on the floor. My legs are leaden.

∽

With morphine, Pop moves into sleep, his breathing unbearably slow. I pull worn-out fentanyl morphine patches from my father's body, replacing them with new ones. I roll him over and gently tear off another plastic patch, grimacing, hoping I won't tear the skin. We are at 200 micrograms now, too much, in my opinion, because Pops is groggy. I pull off three patches, replace them with new ones after hunting everywhere on his back and his stomach for virgin skin. This responsibility worries me; I know nothing about morphine.

We have other concerns now. We need help, not so much for my father, but to help alleviate Mother's surging anxiety. Her worst nightmare is unfolding, and she is not managing well. The Holy Spirit, who has taken night duty since the beginning of chemotherapy, is on his way back to Holland, and now Mom wants twenty-four-hour care for Dad. My father doesn't, and I am in the middle. I tell my father it's just for now, until he gets his strength back. As I talk, I want to believe what I'm saying, but I know in my heart it is unlikely. This dilemma will haunt me forever. I say these things to my father, knowing that as much as I want them to be true, they are not. I don't know what's to come, so I cloak everything I say in hope, hauling out my books of inspiration, the stories of survivors.

"Do you want to know what happened to the other guy we were too afraid to ask about?" I ask my Dad one afternoon.

"I don't know," he says.

"Lael asked the doctor."

I stop and study his face to see whether he wants this information.

"He got so much better, he moved to California."

"What happened then," Dad asks.

"No one's heard from him."

And we're both silent, staring at each other wondering the same thing—is he dead or alive?

My father closes his eyes and beams a half smile, and I wonder what he's thinking.

"Fruits and nuts," I say. One of Dad's old sayings about people who live in California. "Do you remember that?"

"Remember what?"

"What you said about California."

"I don't like California, it's full of fruits and nuts."

"I like it."

"I can't help that," he says. "Everyone who goes to California ends up coming home dressed up like a racehorse. Besides, the earth is unreliable."

"What do you mean unreliable?"

"What I said. I mean unreliable."

"You're a big old stick-in-the-mud."

"I know it," he smiles.

* * *

Finding full-time help is a disaster. While we were in town with the doctors, an agency came out to meet Mother, and they turned down the job.

"What happened," I ask the agency's director over the phone.

She was silent. My mind raced over the possibilities.

"Will you tell me, please," I say. "What happened?"

"I'd rather not."

Bob comes out later that night and we begin to review the possibilities.

"She was drunk," he says, "and probably propositioned the guy."

"Nah," I say. "Really?"

Bob makes a face that says, "Wake up."

We sit in my parents' bedroom. Mother is drunk; Dad says he'd like to go to a nursing home, and then the scene goes black. I don't remember what happens except for what I write down in my journal later that night. "Bobby comes out, grabs Mother around the neck, and throws her drink on the bed. Then he yells at me about how he's not going to quit his job to take care of Dad. I call Lael for reinforcement, and she says she can't come because she has a problem with her pool. I am scheduled to leave, but it's clear that I can't." Can't because I can't leave my father. Cannot. Will not. Refuse to. BD has become my obsession. And besides, it is still raining in Oregon.

The following morning, I begin to maniacally call health care agencies. When I talk to Bob on the phone the next day, he tells me I am in the way.

"Lael and I are on the same page," he says. "Dad must go into a nursing home."

I call Lael again.

Twelve hours later, she walks in the door with Bob, and here we are under this roof all together again, which makes twice in the last thirty years. We stand around the kitchen eating leftovers out of Tupperware tubs, pacing from the fridge to the sink trying to decide what to do.

"Get with it," Bob says again. "Wake up."

I can feel myself growing hysterical so I leave Bob and Lael, and go outside to hide on the outside deck, smoke cigarettes, and call friends on the phone.

The problem is that the sicker Dad gets, the more Mother drinks. The drunker Mother is, the more despondent we become. Not surprisingly, we argue. We argue among ourselves. We stop talking to each other. We argue with Mother. Grinding at each other. *Did he eat that? Did he eat this? Do we have coverage for this day or that day? Who goes shopping? Who plants what flowers where? When? What medications? Laxatives. Dinners. Breakfasts. Doctors' appointments.*

Mother is not happy to have our help. She alternates between calling my sister and me *The Fucking Sisters* or *Tweedledee* and *Tweedledum.* I'm pissed because as the youngest that might mean I'm Tweedledum and I don't want to be. One afternoon while standing in the kitchen, when the Tweedle business is mentioned, I seize on it.

"I'm Tweedledee," I say. "What about Bob? What's he?"

"Tweedlegone," Lael laughs as she moves one arm really quickly in one direction to indicate a person shooting out of sight.

"Tweedle Gone!"

She does the arm thing again. *Ha! Ha! Ha!*

"Nah," Bob says. "You can call me, Tweedle . . ."

He hesitates a moment to think and then blurts, *"Dong! You can call me Tweedledong."*

He smiles, gloating at his special cleverness, while moving his head back and forth like a mental patient, and we all collapse in laughter.

Bob is mostly irritated. One evening when we drive to get a pizza, Bob complains about Lael and me being anxious, too anxious, and gives me the rundown on an engineer's philosophy of control, the details of which I promptly forget. Regardless, I know that what he is saying is wise in the strange way Bob can be, so I put some effort into understanding the analogy. In the end he's talking about how in the world of jet engines and mathematical models, a system can be utterly disrupted when a control overanticipates. No matter how a system tries to anticipate a malfunction, it cannot.

He turns and smiles. I understand he is trying to help me not worry about things I cannot do anything about, but the fact that he uses math and engine systems to illustrate a "control model" as the answer to a question of faith makes me laugh.

By the time Lael and Bob arrive, I have been here for two weeks and I am exhausted. When Lael gets the idea to start planting a few of Dad's gardens, I sit by her and watch her dig small holes for the impatiens in the front and the back according to his detailed instructions. She measures and hems and haws, wanting to draw me in for a hand, but I can't manage to get up off my ass. She is sweet. She lets me sit and smoke while she does all the work.

*　*　*

On one of these afternoons, there are arguments about something ridiculous. Mother and Lael quarrel over who sent who shopping, and I have somehow inserted myself into the middle of it. I run for cover into my father's room, where he lies with his eyes closed. I climb into bed next to him and hear their voices snip and snap. My dad cracks an eye and smiles.

"I just remembered something," he says.

"What's that, Dad?"

"There is no death penalty in Massachusetts."

"What?"

"I just remembered there is no death penalty in Massachusetts."

In the background are the sounds of Mom and Lael going at it, reviewing the last twenty years of injustices.

"Ha! You mean you could have gotten away with offing Mom without being fried."

"I guess so," he laughs. "I blew it."

"You *did* blow it. You blew it big, Daddy-o."

"I know it," he says, closing his eyes and pursing his lips. "I know it."

It is a brilliant afternoon in mid-May, and we lie around and laugh about this death penalty business. Why didn't we think of it before? *Ha! Ho! Ha! Hee!* I look at my Dad, lying there wearing a half smile, the man eternally bemused; even half dead, still the funniest man alive.

13

LOVE STORY

May 1999
Framingham, Massachusetts

Through the years, Monty and Barb tell me that they have argued the same arguments so many times they have them numbered as a kind of shorthand. I've tried to imagine them sitting in their favorite chairs in front of the television shouting numbers, glaring at one another.

God damn it, Barbrrrra. This is the way Pop said her name, skipping a syllable, emphasizing the *rrrr* in bra.

Lael and Bob tell stories about when they were young and Mom and Dad would get bombed and argue. Sometimes, they said, Dad would get so mad he would drag Mom up the stairs by the hair. I never witnessed it, but I saw other arguments. Once Mother pushed a fully fired barbeque into the pool, and I watched Dad, in turn, throw her into the water right after it. In later years, after us kids were out of the house, their too-many-cocktails-after-dinner skirmishes continued, but Mother was the only one drinking and they were silent about the physical details; the only evidence lay in broken bones and the splintered wood of Windsor chairs. Clearly, my parents had an unusual love story. They remind me of the famous couple Martha and George in *Who's Afraid of Virginia Woolf,* and the characters in *The War of the Roses,* a movie they found riotous; it's the only one they ever owned.

"I locked your father out of the house last night," my mother announced one day over the phone. This was the late eighties. Tom and I had just moved to California.

"Get out," I said. "Did not."

"I most certainly did. I locked him out in his underwear."

"Mother!"

"What? *You* live with the bastard. I'm going to take my money and run away."

"Dad?"

"What."

He was outside on the cordless telephone. I imagined that he was walking the deck smoking and pulling leaves off of the pansies planted in old wine casks.

"Is it true?"

"Hell, yes. She locked us both out," he said. "Me and the dog. Poor Inky doesn't understand these types of things."

"It was a nice warm evening, and there was your father out dancing in the moonlight in his skivvies. Thing is, I can't figure out how he got back in. Monty, how'd you do it?"

"I'm not telling."

"There he was off on a skunk hunt in his skivvies, off dancing under the moon for the neighbors to see. He probably got back in through the cellar. I was trying to watch my program. I turned it up so I couldn't hear your father's screams."

"Jesus, Mother. What the hell has gotten into you?"

"You live with him. The man drives me to drink."

"Cheers," I said. "Dad? What are you doing?"

"Painting the gutters."

"How'd you get in?" Mother asked.

"Lay off, I'm not telling."

"Come on."

"I have keys, Blondie, I carry them wherever I go."

"You're full of horse shit. Then why did it take you so long to get in?"

"I was thinking," he said.

"About what?" I asked. There are the sounds of his uneasy breath. "About what?"

"About blowing up the house."

Mother laughed.

"Blowing up the whole fucking thing into bite size pieces." He then fell silent.

"How come you didn't?" I asked.

He didn't answer.

"Dad?"

"What?"

"How come you didn't?"

He didn't answer for what seemed like a long time.

"I couldn't find the gas line in the dark," he finally said.

❧

Have you met my lover? my mother asks one afternoon. I look at her wondering if she actually said what I think she said. We are in the Pine Room, a room of glass at the end of the house overlooking the pool; Pop is napping.

Have you met my lover? she says again.

Lover is pronounced *Luh-va*. It is accentuated by a dramatic index finger raised in the air, the swish and fall of the head.

As my father lays dying, my mother reverts into a fantasy world fueled by gin. It startles me when I realize that she is living in a world where, at times, she is falling in love with The Kid. She lies in her bed one hot afternoon, listening to Stoyan's partially mixed CD, and looking like a lovesick teenager. Incredulous, I look at my father, and then back at her.

"Mother, dahling," I say in a mock Betty Davis accent.

"Yes, dahling, dear."

"I think we should write a play, Mom."

She looks confused.

"A musical," I suggest. " 'If You're Dying of Cancer, Do You Want Us to Tell You?'"

"Oh, no," she says, with her hand over her mouth. "How could you?"

"You said it."

"I didn't."

We begin to laugh.

"You did! Bobby told me."

"I didn't mean it."

It will be a comedy with extravagant dance numbers and lots of sad solos for Mother and me.

Mother perks up.

"Comedy is tragedy, you know," she suggests.

I cross my eyes at her, which has always made her laugh. *As if I don't know.*

If you're dying of cancer, do you want us to tell you is a question Mother actually asked Dad over the winter. Bobby told Lael and me about it at dinner a few nights before. We were sitting in a cheesy Chinese restaurant on Route 9 next to the Sheraton Tara, a huge hotel shaped like a castle. Lael and I sat on the edges of our chairs, huddled over the table to hear the words through Bob's mumbling. More and more, it seems, he talks without moving his jaw.

"She turns to him on the bed and yells, 'Monty, if you're dying of cancer, do want us to tell you?'"

"What did he say?" Lael asks.

"'Hell no'?" I suggest.

Bobby makes a face.

"What did he say?"

"I can't remember."

What do we do now? Keep it a secret?

Mother and I spend one afternoon working on the songs for the musical. We write a blues number called Morphine *(Drip, drip, drip, doo-wop, doo-wop, doo-wop)* and a snazzy jazzy number:

> *The doctors don't talk to the nurses (bewop,*
>   *bewop, bewop),*
> *The nurses don't talk to the doctors.*
> *We can't talk to God,*
> *and God knows he don't talk to us.*

As the afternoon wears on, Mother becomes too drunk to sing so she shrieks instead.

We find an agency that sends women from foreign countries, jet black women from Uganda and Haiti, to help us around the clock. In the early morning, one of them, a very quiet round woman with a beautiful voice, sings lullabies and songs from our musical with Mom and me. We sit in my parents' bedroom in the dark. She fills the air with sweet notes, and then later, taps her foot, nodding her head encouragingly when Mom and I shake out the melody, humming and harmonizing around the kitchen table.

> *The doctors don't talk to the nurses.*
> *The nurses don't talk to them.*
> *We can't talk to God,*
> *And he ain't talking to us.*
> *Oh, no. Oh, God, Don't let him go.*

Mom's hearing aid begins to squeal, and she hands it to Bob.

"You do it," she says. "I can't get the fucking thing in right."

Bob examines it from seemingly every possible angle, fiddles, and then in one quick motion sticks it into Mother's ear. When it begins to squeal again, he smacks her on the side of the head in the same way someone would pound a radio that had static.

"Ouch," Mother's hand reaches to her ear and she looks up at him searching for some sort of explanation.

Bob grins sheepishly, and I cannot help it, I begin to howl in laughter. They join in and we disintegrate into hyenas, laughing, crying, gut-wrenching, fall-on-the-floor, cannot stop hysteria.

Later, I watch Mom come wheeling around the corner into the bedroom. Dad looks up and smiles as wide as a child, his eyes bright. There is such a spark at that moment, a recognition that instantaneously zips decades into the past. They reach for each other's hands, and Mother pushes him over to sit down on the bed.

I remember them embracing each other through the years, holding hands, hugging each other in their sleep, holding onto one another in a surf break on a beach in Maui, my only vacation with them anywhere. This was in the eighties during Mother's second sober period. They howl at the force of the water trying to overtake them. And for an instant, the years of misunderstandings and disappointments vanish. This is grace, I think. This dying business is about endings, yes, but also quite possibly its difficulty carves a tiny space in people's hearts for something new.

14

HANDS

May 1999
Framingham, Massachusetts

There is something about my father's hands and feet. They endure. He loses hundreds of pounds—his body grows into only bones, his face melts into the unrecognizable expression of a tormented old man, but his fingers, those lovely stubs cut off at the ends, the rough, rosy palms of his hands that reach, mend, fiddle, worry, and repair, remain unchanged. I know them well from years of study—I have watched them countless times, wrapped around car steering wheels, knocking nails into things, pulling wires from underneath cars, turning small gadgets around like miniature planets.

His feet also stay the same. They remain loyal, shaped like the webbed feet of the ducks on the Boston Common, as wide and odd as old ladies' fans. They are hard to fit, hard to find comfortable shoes for, but they stand by him, holding him upright, stubborn, steadfast, planted so dearly and squarely on the earth. These are the things that do not give in easily, these feet or these hands. They do not relinquish their place in this world happily. They do not want to let go.

∞

On a Sunday afternoon in May, I lie next to my father and watch him breathe. It is hot and quiet, and he uses every part of his body to accomplish the feat. Earlier that morning, while he sat on the side of the bed having a meal, I pointed to the strange contortions his upper body made with every breath. Lael and Bob, standing in the doorway watching, nodded. They now knew what I had been trying to tell them about Dad's breathing being labored.

"This butter makes me so unhappy," my father said. The knife slipped off the hard cold surface of the butter and onto the plate with a clinking sound as my father's upper body jerked in one full motion, as if fending off sleep.

"Hard butter has always made me unhappy."

He turned and smiled, and I smiled back, because I too have had a long-standing problem with hard butter.

His hands then maneuvered around his meal effortlessly, from this to that.

"I never thought about getting old," my father tells me later that afternoon. "I never thought I would."

"Did you ever feel old?"

"Nope, never did. Not until this friggin' cancer."

His face tightens and his body shudders, as if his nerves no longer reach their ends.

"I think it's good to get mad, Dad."

"Fucking cancer," he says.

"Be gone! Be gone." I try the magical circle thing with my hand, then shoot up out of bed and punch the air.

"Take that! Boom!" I say.

"The last thing I ever wanted was a long, lingering illness," he says. "I always thought my father did it right. Get up on Saturday morning to do the chores. Go grocery shopping and keel over." He hesitates. "Kaput."

He purses his lips, patting the bed in a solid, sweeping rhythm.

"Hey, have you seen the card from Gary?" he asks. Gary, the son of my father's brother, is a Christian minister.

"No, I don't think so," I say.

He continues to pat the bed, finds the card and hands it to me. It is a sweet card, a dear, sincere good-bye card, but it seems odd.

Dear Uncle Robert, it reads. My cousin writes about how he appreciates what he remembers of my dad, his great sense of humor, and then launches into a treatise about God.

You and I have never had an opportunity to talk about God, he writes. *Maybe this is a good time. I realized I was a sinner 23 years ago and though I knew God could punish me, I knew Christ had died for our sins.*

Incredulous, I hold the card up.

"It's the Jesus died for our sins part that loses me," I say.

"Leave him alone," my father says. "He is sincere."

"Sincere?" I say. "He *is* a sinner. The way he used to swim underwater to look at Mimi Whitcomb's boobs."

"Leave him alone."

"Are you nuts?"

"He is sincere," my father repeats.

There are many differences in my father. He is very pale, and his eyes are larger than before.

∞

At dusk, Stoyan sweeps in, dressed in one of my father's dress shirts, a blue and white striped Brooks Brothers button-down. The sleeves are rolled up because his arms are much longer than my father's. He is holding a Foster's beer and is beside himself with joy, having just finished recording his first CD with a piano player and friend from Bulgaria, Daddy Long Legs. He smiles as he keeps slugging back the enormous blue can. He runs around the house, full of himself. I hear him talk excitedly and then, in response to his stories, a few delighted hoots from Pop. Stoyan is great entertainment for Pop, who seems to get an endless kick out of him and his youthful antics. It is a nice respite.

A day later, Dad, Lael, Bob, and I spend eight hours in the emergency room because my father's breathing has worsened. The visiting nurse insists we go to the ER at the Boston hospital. When we arrive, Dad is dry heaving and gagging in the waiting area, so we are taken to a small room where a scowling nurse snarls at us.

"What is this?" she impatiently asks. "Are you having trouble breathing or throwing up?"

My father only looks at her. He is trying to smile, but he is so sick and so scared, he heaves again.

She moves her hand in a circle as if signaling, *Hurry up, would you? Please?*

We give her the rundown. He is a Dana-Farber patient

sent to ER on the advice of the visiting nurse and his physician.

Seven hours later, we leave. It is one in the morning. My father does not have pneumonia, but has another prescription for Percodan.

Two days later, we are back. This time at Dana-Farber getting fluids and more chemotherapy for my father's pump. We have found sores in his mouth. We ask the doctor to take a look at them. Deep sores accompanied by a white fungus move around his tongue and down his throat. The doctor takes a quick peek.

"They seem fine," he says.

We say, no, they are not fine and urge him to get a light. He does. He tells us that we need to hold off on the chemo for a week. Pops is dehydrated so we hang out for hours as he gets pumped up with intravenous fluids and we meet with a new pain management specialist, who prescribes a series of new medications.

It is on this afternoon that I track down The Oncologist. We meet in a small room and sit across from one another. He gently tries to tell me that he too is very concerned, that Dad is not looking good, and though we need to wait for the CAT scan in about a week to know anything for certain, he suspects the disease is progressing very quickly.

"I never asked you what happened to the others on the trial?" I say.

Despite his smile, The Oncologist looks sad. He appears to be sitting on the corner of his chair, his white laboratory coat falling to the sides to reveal gray flannel trousers. His hands are small, girlish, and fine.

"Well," he says, "the disease progresses."

Once he has said it, he looks as if he is waiting for something to happen.

I stare at him for a long moment and begin to cry, sputtering apologies. He tilts his head and nods, helplessly.

On my way back to Dad, his nurse takes me aside to give me details on how to help Dad die at home. "Pain management is very difficult," she says. "You need to talk to the doctor to get him to agree to admit your Dad in case you run into any problems so you can put him under until . . ."

I look at her mouth. "Until?"

She nods and I understand her to mean until he dies. She sits behind the counter of the nurses' station trying to act all business. I am silent, looking at her, and we stay that way staring at each other for a while as I hunt around for a place to hide all this new information, a place I don't have to see anymore today. I am not ready for any of this. I do not want my father to die, and as long as I can sit with him, hold his hand, and watch him breathe, my hope will stay.

"Get that organized now," she advises, "before it becomes a problem. I know. I had my father die at home, and it was a nightmare."

I study her some more and think about how pretty she is and how happy she'll be once she gets her in-the-ground swimming pool.

I walk around the corner and find my father asleep behind a curtained treatment area. He lies on a gurney with tubes moving from his shoulder portacath to miscellaneous plastic bags of fluids hanging from the IV stand. Bob and Lael are wandering, so I just sit and stare at my Dad for a few minutes until he opens an eye. Just one.

"Hey, Pops."

"Hello there, kid," he says.

Elsewhere in chairs are other patients, dressed in scarves and in hats, who chat while hooked up to chemo. I learn later that these folks look relatively good because they are not fighting gastrointestinal cancers, which are renowned for being stubborn and difficult to treat.

That night at home, Dad is feeling better. After dinner, we plug in The Kid's new CD, *Spirit On*. The music is a wild mix of Middle Eastern, Bulgarian folk, and rap. I wear my father's Worcester Polytech Institute baseball cap sideways on my head and dance around the bedroom.

"What do you know," Dad says. "It's pretty good."

"That's good," Lael laughs, "because you're a major investor."

Ha! Dad hoots. *Ho!*

They banter like the old days and have a great laugh while I dance around in front of the bed. The music continues, but I sit to write down the list of my father's new medications. I plan to return to Oregon the following day for a few days and need to be sure Lael and Bob know what's happening. I look up to collect my thoughts as I write and when I turn to my father, his hands are in the air and he is squealing.

"Dad," I yell, jumping up. "Dad!"

His face sets into a horrendous grimace.

As I run to my father's side, Mom and Lael scream, running in circles.

"Call 911."

My father continues to squeal. His hands, raised above his

head, are convulsing. His face contorts, his eyes moving around their sockets at wild speeds as he blinks madly. I hold him down on the bed as his body bucks.

"Dad," I yell. "Breathe. One. Two. Three. Breathe."

He continues having seizures, his legs jumping and his face contorted. I am yelling at my sister. *Call 911. Call 911.* A second passes, my father stops moving. His eyes are ablaze, and blood drips from his mouth. I am frightened that he is dead. My mother stands behind me.

"Monty," she says. "Monty. I'm here. Easy. Settle. Monty, easy. Breathe."

I jump up and look away. I am terrified that we have arrived at the instant when my father's life will be yanked away in one final blow. I run to the other room to talk to the ambulance people on the phone. A few minutes later, I am standing in front of them shouting. I yell about what's happened and shout all his medications, over and over and over and over, suspecting the seizure has something to do with the new medicine.

I am hysterical. I keep yelling Dad's long list of medications, the long list of conditions. The long list of everything. "He is diabetic," I scream. "He is being treated for stomach cancer. He is . . ."

I look over at my father stretched out on the gurney; his face is completely different. His eyes are enormous, and they have changed color. They are no longer green, they are blue, and he looks as if he has just slept for a hundred years.

I make telephone calls trying to locate The Oncologist, and Lael rides in the ambulance to the Framingham Hospital. When I arrive at the ER fifteen minutes later, Dad is awake but silent. I kiss him and ask questions.

"Do you know who I am?"

"Yep, you're Lee," he says.

I spend the rest of the time yelling at the nurses. The on-call doctor and I are old friends, having spent hours together two weeks before. After waiting for some time, he tells us the CAT scan is broken and Dad needs to be transferred to Boston. We insist the ER doctor make all the calls so that Dad can be admitted without having to wait again in the Brigham emergency room but, despite his and our efforts, we have no such luck.

Bob rides in the ambulance with Dad this time while Lael and I drive together, which means that because Lael drives, we take all the wrong turns before finally getting on the Turnpike.

There, at the Brigham emergency room, we wait up most of the night before he is admitted. For hours they have been suspecting a brain tumor. By the time we receive the news that there is no brain tumor, it is three in the morning. Bobby and I have curled up and fallen asleep in the chairs of the waiting room.

"C'mon, you guys," Lael says. "There's no brain tumor. They're taking him up."

We move through the hallways in a daze. Before we slept, we had been causing a ruckus. After another eight-hour wait, we are pissed off. Our father is clearly in deep trouble, and everything takes forever. An orderly begins to wheel him out of his treatment station in the ER but forgets to take the oxygen tube out of his nose so it is torn out with a snap.

We follow the gurney, his chart hanging on the back. Lael keeps pulling at my shirtsleeve and pointing to it. I pick it up. Many things are written on it, but what she wants me to see is: *Family is anxious.*

"Not anxious," she says as we crowd into the elevator around Dad's gurney. "Appalled." She hands me a pen and I cross out "anxious" and write it in red. *Not anxious. Appalled.*

We tell Dad, and he smiles, happy we're causing trouble, whatever that means. Pop's brain is scrambled. He does not know the first thing about what is happening. In fact, the seizure erased part of his hard drive, so he doesn't even remember he has cancer.

The seventh-floor cancer wing is a deathwatch. It's three or four in the morning, and family members mill about. It is dark, it is dreary, and all I can do is replay my father's seizure over and over in my head. I walk around the floor and feel sick with the knowledge that this is the place where they put people when they're dying. Not at all like the sunny, hermetically sealed Dana-Farber rooms we visited the week before.

"I don't know what your mother will do if I hit the crapper," my father says the next day. He is very happy. The doctors tell us he is high because of one of the drugs. "I don't know what your mother will do with the house if I hit the crapper." He laughs and lifts his head to the side and says, *Weeeeeeee!*

We sit with him, happy he is happy. He squeals and giggles and pinches and *oohs* and *ahs* and when the nurses come in or the family in the next bed sneaks a peek at us through the curtain, my father goes, *Boo!*

"Boo!"

His head bobs along the trajectory of a nurse's ass cruising by and I say, "Dad! You are a dirtball."

"You're damn right," he says, and he lifts his head up and to the side and squeals with delight, laughing, and holding what would be his belly, if there was anything there.

"Do they even know what's wrong with me?" he asks. Everything about my father is disjointed, like a living Picasso. Nothing is connecting.

"What's this thing in the neck?" he says tugging at the portacatheter.

"Dad," I say. "Do you remember anything about the last six months?"

"No," he says, laughing. "Not a thing."

A little later we bring Richie in, a visiting nurse who took care of Pop on Saturdays during the winter when we were not there.

"Dad, you remember Richie," I say.

"Never seen the man before in my life," he says.

∞

A day later, the doctors tell my father that the cancer is growing. They never use the words: Die, to die. Dying. Death. They tell us other things that mean he is dying, without ever saying it. Bob writes them all down, one after another in order, in an outline. The chemotherapy is not working. The tumors are growing. There is nothing they can do. All these doctors—the oncologist, the hospital doctor, the resident, the intern, the doctor on call, the other resident no one's ever heard of, and the social worker no one has ever met. All these professionals Bob numbers in his notes (Doctors No. 1 and No. 2 and so on) come to tell my father that he is dying without ever saying the word. All these strangers are here to tell my father that nothing is working anymore. What they do is recommend supportive therapy, which my father misinterprets as therapy that will keep him alive for a long time. When I see his misunderstanding, I look over at Lael and Bob standing on the other side of the bed and see they are crying too.

The Oncologist does all the talking and the others, Doctors No. 1 and No. 2, Residents No. 1 and No. 2, the Intern, and the Social Worker, stand at the foot of the bed with their hands behind their backs. Lael, Bob, and I look at each other, at Dad, and then at the lineup of medical professionals, not quite understanding the purpose of their presence except for—perhaps—legal purposes. They know we are furious. All morning, I have been telephoning up and down the chain of command, yelling at each and every one, because it seemed impossible to get any information about anything. But none of that is mentioned. Instead, we smile courteously at one another as The Oncologist sits close to Dad and lists the options of other chemo trials available, none that appears to be especially effective, followed by the final, inevitable option of calling hospice and doing nothing.

I hold onto my father's legs while the doctor tells him this.

My father lies back and shrugs his shoulders.

"That would be like giving up the ghost," he says.

"Yes, it would," the doctor says.

The Oncologist continues talking about hospice and the Do Not Resuscitate (DNR) order that needs to accompany signing onto the program.

My father looks at all of us and smiles sadly as he stretches his palm out in front of him and pretends to be some official reading it.

"Sorry, kid, you're not on the list," he says, shrugging and looking at us, trying to manage a weak smile.

We all look at him—mouths open, hearts broken.

"We'll let you think about it and talk to your family," The Oncologist says. "I'll be back."

Then all the doctors turn and stream out of the room almost in formation like a skating team. My father takes a breath, his eyes as firm as pins, his mouth almost flapping, speechless.

I follow The Oncologist out into the hallway to ask him the same question I've been asking all along: *What does this mean? What happens?* How does it happen? My face feels drenched and swollen. I keep swiping at tears. He smiles weakly, his hands jammed into the pockets of his white coat. "Well," he says, his breath catching as if he might break apart. "Well," he begins again, "his systems will slowly shut down and he'll stop breathing."

I look at him and try to say something, but I cannot form the words. I nod my thanks and turn away and return to my father's room, where we all stand around and cry while trying not to. We have fought so hard for months, and now there is nothing left to fight for. There is nothing else to do. I feel so deflated after all of this yelling and running around and staying up all night, and watching and hoping and asking questions, the keeping track of this and that. It's over.

The doctor talks about hospice and sending him home, but we don't know anything about hospice. The social worker—who was not our normal social worker—did not know the right hospice to call. (Our normal social worker worked only Monday, Tuesday, and Wednesday and this was a Friday.) Or maybe it was the nurse who did not know. We weren't sure who didn't know.

∞

"I wish I had lilacs like that," The Oncologist says when he stops by later. He pushes his nose into the vase full of purple lilacs we brought from Dad's garden. Us kids had given Mom and Dad three lilac bushes for an anniversary present not too long ago and now they are in full bloom.

"I can't get my lilacs to grow like that," the doctor says.

"Really," Dad says. "When do you prune them?"

The doctor tells Dad something I can't really hear, and Dad yells, "Oh! No! You're pruning the blossoms. You've got to prune after they flower."

Right now giving this young man a primer on pruning, Dad is in full glory. He is animated. He is strong and happy to share this information. When the doctor leaves, I mention to Dad that perhaps we should have asked the doctor about his gardening expertise. "Maybe we should have said, 'If we had known that you were such a lousy gardener, perhaps we wouldn't have selected you as our oncologist?'"

"Nah, we wouldn't tell him that." Dad says. "It would only hurt his feelings."

Lael and I pick Dad up from the hospital the next morning to take him home. When we arrive, we hear from one of the nurses on the floor that hospice is closed on weekends. So we are on our own—no visiting nurses, no hospice nurses, and though we don't want Dad to come home under these circumstances, we have no choice because they told him he was going home, and he has been getting dressed since seven o'clock, waiting for us to pick him up.

When we get to Dad's room, he is ecstatic to see us, though he has a bruised arm. The nurse tells us he fell out of bed, but Dad says, "Did not! I slid!" In any event, he is fine and can barely wait to get his ass in the wheelchair. We pile all his belongings on his lap, take his long list of medications, and wheel him down the hall, into the elevator, and outside into a brilliant morning. Next to him on the sidewalk is a new mother with a brand-new baby wrapped in pink. Behind her are bundles of colorful helium-filled balloons. We all hunt for the new baby hidden by blankets, and the mother holds her up for us to see. My father turns to me and back to the baby and laughs. "Will you look at that brand-new baby." It is a sight. A new baby stepping into the world next to a man who is stepping out.

∞

Later that day, I'm on my way back to the house from somewhere, I take a detour to the liquor store to buy a bottle of expensive red wine. That evening Bob and I sit down with it at the kitchen table. I pound a glass and immediately feel a nice buzz, and looking across the table I notice Big Brother is also wearing a glow.

"So what I am going to do," Bob says, "is drill tiny holes in all the glasses so whenever she reaches for her little martini, it will just dribble away."

He laughs as he mimes the scene. He picks up a glass. Uses his hand to mimic the actual drilling, then shows the stream of liquid where the drink will dribble, and feigns the presumed face of bewilderment of our mother once she sees her drink slowly dribble away.

I get more wine and we continue to drink as the sky grows dark with night. My head feels numb and sentimental. Bob picks at the table cloth and then builds mountains out of the bottles of vitamins Pop never took. He lifts his empty glass. I fill it.

"I'm loaded," I say.

"He laughs. "Maybe she's onto something. She might be onto something."

"Definitely."

We raise our glasses, toast to nothing.

Lael does not drink, hasn't for over ten years. She organizes instead. She has spent the last months and weeks organizing drawers, buying a new lounge chair for BD. She's also bought new linens, pajamas, cookware, and in the last week a new refrigerator. She is amazing. The world could be falling around us, and Lael would be organizing the piles of rubble.

Early on in Dad's illness, one of her first projects is installing a phone system with three lines, a system sophisticated enough that it could supply an office of one hundred workers. The only problem is Mother can't learn how to use it. She keeps punching the wrong line. She picks up the receiver. Punches the button. Swears. Punches. Swears.

For much of our time at home together when Dad begins to die, Lael and I power walk around the block in the morning for our daily review. Lael and I have always had great fun playing this game I call Doom, because even though the world is full of optimists, we believe on some level that it is our mission to talk about how hopeless everything is. *Doom. Doom. Doom.* Sometimes when we play Doom, we shake our heads in agreement, and grunt our sympathies. Other times, we disagree. We argue about this and that. We argue about the hopelessness of the situation. *How hopeless is hopeless?* We argue about our fucked up Mother. *How fucked up the health care system is, how incompetent the doctors are or are not. . . .* We argue about our different impressions, resolutions, experience. We differ on a lot of points but after a lifetime of little sister deference, a lifetime of agreeing, now, as my father dies, it suddenly becomes critical to make my dissent known. The problem is it is almost impossible for me to argue with Lael or Bob, but I do. Finally, I do, and it is awful. It is painful. It is terrible. Some days I can't believe how such perfect human beings as my loving brother and sister could have turned into such complete assholes.

A few days after Dad gets home, Lael and I go to hospice and sit in an office with a hospice nurse. We are both near hysteria. Dad has been sent home with no support and we need to get him professional care as soon as possible, but we don't know the first thing about it. I am trying to talk to the hospice nurse about their care, and Lael keeps interjecting comments about how horrible the medical system is because of everything we've been through over the last few months, but also because no one contacted hospice. She is right in her assessment, but it is so hopeless I feel like my brain is going to explode.

"Lael, stop," I say. And I look at her and know I have committed a sin. She is furious. Her arms cross in front of her. When we leave the building she reads me the riot act. How dare I interrupt her? How dare I? I try to explain.

There is no use in taking on the whole fucking system. Our argument lasts the few miles home, and ends with her slamming the car door, spitting. "You're fucking crazy."

The next morning Bob, Mom, and I are waiting for hospice to come. Mom and I talk about it, what will be required of us, as Bob looks through the Yellow Pages at nursing care options. Mother turns to me and says, "I don't know if I can do this."

"This is your decision, Mom," I say. "Maybe we should talk more. . . ."

There is always the option of a nursing home, not that Bob or I think it's a good one at the moment.

"You know," Bob says, "Not every comment needs a response."

"Bob, I try to respect your way of handling yourself. I would appreciate if you would respect mine."

"Great, then when you have her really wound up—"

"Then, you handle it," I say and leave the room.

Later, when I'm trying to talk to him about something, he says, "Lie down," as if he's talking to a dog.

Mother is drunk. Dad is dying. And the three of us disintegrate into chaos around the question of hospice. It is brief, but awful. We dig our heels into the earth as if we have a vote, as if our decisions will make some difference.

❀

By the time the coordinating nurse arrives to set up hospice care, five days later, my father has decided that he does not want to sign the Do Not Resuscitate order. He wants to be resuscitated, and no one blames him. But the DNR part is key to hospice. To help someone to die, they must admit they are dying. But Dad is not admitting that he is dying or sometimes he just forgets. No one has the heart to tell him, and no one will sign it for him. We all talk with the hospice nurse for hours. I sit in a chair next to the bed, and lay my head on a pillow next to him as he strokes my hair.

"So, Dad, let's say you are resuscitated? What if you cannot breathe on your own? How long do you want to be that way?"

"You decide," he says. After a family round of "Who Will Decide?" we let it go, arranging for a bridge program leading up to hospice care with the MetroWest Hospice, which is an informal hospice. They provide the same nurses and emotional support for the family, but we are instructed to call 911 if Pop encounters any kind of medical emergency.

A day passes, and Dad slowly begins to reconnect all that is happening. I hear him on the telephone with his brothers and friends.

"How am I?" he says. "Lousy. The chemotherapy isn't working."

There is an afternoon full of wild thunderstorms. It is rainy and humid, the air is white and thick. I wake from a nap and find Lael and Bob collapsed on the couch together in the Pine Room giggling and reminiscing about meals; Dad trying to make them eat sauerkraut. Every time he did they would gag. And then Lael had stories about constantly being excused from the dinner table because she would get bad cases of the giggles that would cause her to slip under the table in a fit of laughter.

I sit down and try to join in, but realize that they are

part of a completely different family than I. They grew up together, for many years as best friends, and share countless stories of childhood. They also know another mother and father, who, for some time, were actually parents, who were for some time almost whole.

In the next room, my father gets a sponge bath by his nurse's aide, a lovely woman I refer to as Dad's Haitian princess. She is beautiful and dear and takes very good care of Dad. She rolls him over, and with a hot towel she painstakingly cleans every inch of my father as the sky booms and the rain pours.

When the thunder cracks, I remember my jokes about Dad being thunder and mother lightning. I ask my father in a whisper, "Hey Dad, is that you?" and he smiles and nods. He is completely out of it because of the high doses of morphine he needs to control the pain of the tumors, but he looks so fine, so clean, dressed in his blue and white pinstripe pajamas that Lael bought him.

This is what he talks about: There is a cat in the television. His mother stands in the corner. He can taste her homemade root beer of years ago and remembers racing his younger brothers to drink the last bottle of root beer. By accident, he drank vinegar instead! He had a famous throat then. He didn't even need to swallow.

That rainy afternoon, Richie comes for a visit. This time Dad recognizes him. Even though Richie's not on duty, he checks Dad's vital signs. They chat about nothing, and then Richie asks Dad about hospice.

"I just don't understand what the benefit is," my father says. He sits up in bed, and Richie sits across the room in an overstuffed chair, his forehead shiny from the heat. He keeps pushing his glasses up his little nose.

"Excuse me, sir," Richie says leaning forward. "The benefits? You are dying. You do understand that. The treatment is not working."

He is the only person who has said these words to my father: *You are dying.* I roll them around in my head. I am sitting in a chair across from Richie. He is as small as me, barely five four with dark skin, eyes and hair. At some point over the winter, Mom and Dad learned that Richie had leukemia as a child. My parents are on the bed. My father slips his shoulders, purses his lips, but doesn't say a word.

I climb into the bed between him and Mother and take his hand.

"Are you frightened, sir," Richie asks. "Do you want to talk about it?"

"No," my father says, looking at his fingers. "Not really, but it is the unknown."

"Not like you get any postcards from the Beyond," I say.

"Hey, Monty," Mother yells. "What are we planting in those barrels? Cosmos? Bachelor buttons? Petunias? Aster?"

"No, not aster," my father yells back. "And you gotta get the blue bachelor buttons."

"What blue?" my mother yells.

"The blue blue," my father yells.

Richie and I look at one another. Case closed.

∞

I lie awake at night wondering if he is awake too, trying to squeeze in the last minutes as the tumors grow inside him.

I imagine he can feel them now, each one, and their achy, restless centers. By now, his liver tumor has doubled back, dying, outstripping even its own ingenious blood supply, now 10 cm by 7 cm, larger than a pack of smokes, and there are others: in the stomach, the kidney, the lung, the heart, and in his mottled bones.

One night when I go check on him, he must feel me take his hand and squeeze, but he doesn't wake. "Dad? Can you hear me? Can you hear me?"

A few days later, the hospice nurse tells me he is not dying. Not yet. It is a good time for me to go home for a spell. Not long. A week or so.

"He's not actively dying," she whispers, "you need a break. I'll call you if there is any change."

It is a peculiar concept. My father is dying, but not actively. No one knows anything about where we are in this process. We are given books so we know the signs of active dying, and he is not doing that. We are told to watch for certain signs that tell us the time is near, like sleeping and not eating and talking about things we cannot see. And the fact remains that he keeps forgetting this; he keeps forgetting that he has cancer. He keeps forgetting that he is dying.

The day before I leave, I am completely torn apart but believe it is an act of faith to go.

"He could go all summer. We don't know," the nurse says. "You've been here a month. You need to take a break."

So to let my Dad know all is well, I tell him I'm going home to check in on Tommy and the animals. We talk about planting the whiskey barrels I had bought a few weeks before.

"You need to bore some holes in the bottom and get those screens in," he says.

"I know it, but I'm not sure how."

"You go downstairs and get the drill and a bore about . . ." He pushes his fingers in the air about an inch apart to denote the approximate diameter, about an inch. "Oh, I'd say, about so big."

"What drill?"

"One of the drills in the box."

"Where are the bores?"

"You don't remember? You got to look. Next to the bits on the bench."

"Where are the screens?"

He has to think about this. I watch a finger come to his lips and rest a spell as his eyes focus on the ceiling.

"Do you know the old wooden tool chest under the bottles of parts?"

"Yeah."

"You'll find a piece of screen you can use to cut out in there. I believe the second drawer. You want to make him, oh I'd say . . ." His fingers indicate the size. "Say, that big?"

"So how do I space the holes?"

"Do you have a pencil?" he asks.

I find a pen and paper, and Dad draws a circle and colors it in, then draws several smaller circles around it.

"Like that," he hands me the pad.

All morning, I lap back and forth from his workshop to his bed, double-checking details. The drill. The bores. Connecting the bore to the drill, which I insist he has to do. He clicks it together like a pro, and after I drill the holes in the barrel I bring it into him and turn it upside down for him to see.

"Perfect," he announces, giving the okay signal with his fingers. "Absolutely perfect, Kid," and he smiles a big one.

I am ecstatic to see him smile. I climb onto the bed and kiss his face all over like I did when I was small and my Daddy-o, overwhelmed with the awkwardness of affection, laughs and pushes me away. I move away, sit, and take his hand, watching as his other reaches for me, his fingers curling around my free forearm now stretched across his stomach, moving to my wrist, poking at my bracelets, to my hand, straightening the stones on my engagement and wedding rings.

"I love you, Dad."

"I love you, too, Lee. I do."

15

FLOATING

Memorial Day 1999
Stevenson, Washington

On a hot summer evening at a cabin on the Columbia River, my husband sinks his head under water in the hot tub, and when he comes up for air his short hair falls onto his forehead creating a peculiar bang in the same way my father's hair fell years earlier when he swam, surfacing from the turquoise depths of our swimming pool, his arms swaying underwater to keep him afloat, his mouth dipping under the water line, spraying great plumes of water like a whale. He was a great swimmer and had perfected a beautiful crawl stroke, which he liked to show off at every opportunity.

As a child, I watched him carefully, adoringly: Diving a crisp dive, his feet perfect, close together, he went deep, his short, strong New England legs bending, pushing him off the bottom, he rose to the surface, emerging with a great boom of delight. *Ahhhhhh!* He swam backward, his wet hair pasted on his forehead in a bang, and then rolled over, his body face down, his arms splayed out to his sides—dead man's float. *Do it again! Daddy! Do it again, Daddy. Do it again!*

My birthday occurs during this short break back in Oregon and Tom has brought me to a cabin on the Columbia River to windsurf. Dad has seen the Columbia River Gorge only in pictures, but it is a place I tell him about and a place where I think about him so intently that he inhabits my time here. At night, I dream about him. During the day, I think about him as I stare into sun glimmering on the river, the evergreens, the rocks; or smell the pondy water of the river. It all reminds me of the lake in New Hampshire he adored.

I'm supposed to be windsurfing, but I am lackadaisical about it. Instead, I sail to the middle of the river, and fall into the water, and float. Holding the sail above me, I fill it with the wind and then sink my head underwater to stop the sound. While my father is dying but not dying, I listen to the sound of the wind in a river thousands of miles away from him. I let go of the sail and slip under the water into the breathless and silent world of the dead.

On my birthday, I phone home from the telephone booth outside the cabins and talk to Bob, who has taken to mumbling almost full time. He is flipped out, yet only provides half the story in order not to flip me out. We review medications, and he downplays everything. We argue. Pop is on a new type of oral morphine and is too sedated; Bob is splitting pills, messing up the time release.

There is a smell that Lael and Bob talk about, a sweet pungent smell like lilies that the Haitian princess terms the "smell of death," but the hospice nurse tells us that it is the smell of cancer. It comes and goes. It's there and then disappears. I talk to my father.

"Dad?"

"Hmm," he says, his brain garbled on drugs.

"I love you, Dad."

Silence.

"I'll be there in a few days," I say.

"I miss you," he says and drops the phone.

That morning, Mother told me that Dad had asked about a helicopter on the deck and told her he was too young to go to school, so I know the time is near, and this is the thing that startles me: everything instantly becomes geared toward dying. Only a few days before, every thought and action was geared toward life. On Monday, all my quiet moments prayed for the miracle of life. By Saturday, everything I think about is arranged around helping my father die in peace.

I miss you, he says.

The next day I climb on a plane and fly across the entire United States knowing I am going home to watch my father die. It is late afternoon and still quite hot when I arrive and find him in a sitting room off the living room. He lies in a hospital bed surrounded by windows overlooking the pool and the back field.

In the five days I've been gone, everything has changed. My father now wears a death mask. He sleeps with his mouth and eyes open, his eyes a different color than before, now always blue. He has stopped eating. The family stands around him. Mother is in a chair nearby. A new health care worker for this Saturday only, an Irish woman, sits on the couch engrossed in one of Mother's paperback romance novels.

"Kissy Face is here," Bob says.

My father turns to me and smiles but does not say anything. I kiss him all over his face, holding onto his hands.

"Daddy-o!"

"We've been telling him all day, Kissy Face is coming," Bob says. I kiss him again, and my father reaches for me.

Lael grabs my father's toes.

> *This little piggy went to the market.*
> *This little piggy stayed home.*
> *This little piggy had roast beef.*
> *This little piggy had none.*
> *And this little pig went weeewee all the way home.*

My father giggles and then stares off into space.

"Do you want anything to eat?" I ask.

He shakes his head.

"How 'bout some coffee ice cream?"

He turns to the health care worker and smiles.

"Yeah," he says like an excited child, moving his shoulders up and down. She gets up and, when she returns, she feeds him, another new event.

Later, Bob, Susan, Lael, and I feast on a meal Susan has prepared in celebration of her and Bob's twenty-fifth wedding anniversary. We sit on the back deck where I can watch my father through the glass doors. I cannot tell if he sees us or is staring at his own reflection in the glass. I look at the others sitting around the table, and then back at my father on the other side of the glass. He is so very much alone and no matter how hard I try, I cannot imagine what he is thinking.

He talks about girls in pink dresses picking daisies in the meadow, an old woman selling tickets. That, along with the helicopter on the deck and not eating, indicates that it could be a matter of a day. The hospice people say when someone stops eating, they are living on spiritual energy alone. When they begin talking about transportation or seeing things and people who we cannot see, they already have one foot in the spiritual world.

The following day, Bob and Susan take off for the graduation of a niece, and Lael prepares to return home to California for a respite. She has been here for a month, and as a prime target for Mother's rage, she is emotionally wrung out. She lies with Dad a few hours before she leaves. Since Dad is clearly not long for this world, I am hoping she changes her mind and stays, but she doesn't. I am near hysteria as she gathers her things; it seems clear that she will never see him again. Over past months, Lael has told me repeatedly that Dad left her long ago. I suppose it's true, but the declaration leaves me utterly confused. To me, Lael could never do any wrong; she seemed the center of Dad's eye. Sometimes it's striking how different our versions of the same events are. I watch her walk out to the limousine and I want to run out, grab her, and pull her back: *Please, please, please don't go.*

Minutes after the arrival of her airport limousine, Mom, Dad, and I receive a visit from the hospice minister, who talks individually to each of us. The minister is a colossal-size man, and we sit together outside on the deck. He talks about forgiveness. I smoke cigarettes and cry. We hold hands and he prays out loud for my father. He talks about the Lord and about Mercy and Peace and Forgiveness and all these things that mean that my father will die soon. I ask the minister about Dad's faith, about coming back to talk to Dad, and the minister tells me that Dad said his family is his support. After I show him to the car, I climb into bed with my mom and Dad and listen to them sleep for a long time. Mother makes quick little pig-like snorts, but my father makes gusty hollow sounds, like the wind of all of time is rushing through him.

Bob and Susan return that evening, and we eat strawberries from Susan's family's farm. Bob chops up the morphine pills and, much to my father's delight, mixes them with strawberries and ice cream. It is Sunday, and we sit with Dad watching *Antiques Roadshow,* his favorite TV program. Mother lies beside him, sound asleep, and I lie down between them. My brother darts in and out. My father is alert, present.

"Hey, Dad," Bob says. "Remember when we sank the boat in Lake Cochituate?"

My father laughs hard and I think back on this story, not remembering if I was there or if it was something I heard about.

"Remember when I drove the car into the freshly plowed field the night of my senior prom and sank it up to the axle?"

And again my father laughs, shaking his head.

The remembering and laughter go on all evening. My father lies with a magazine over his chest. He is here now, and as I watch him remembering this or that, it does not occur to me that this is the end; that this will be the last time we will do this. I stupidly think he might be gaining strength; maybe he'll last all summer. But the hospice books talk about a stage when the dying wake up one last time before they move on.

"I'm out of gas," Dad tells me that night.

"You're out of gas?"

"The car is out of gas."

"Dad, *you* are out of gas."

"No," he says somewhat insistently. "The car is out of gas. It's on the side of the road. Get Bob."

"Bob," I yell. "Come here."

Bob comes in.

"Dad says the car is out of gas."

"What, Dad?"

"Bob, the car is out of gas," Dad says quite insistently. "It's on the side of the road and I don't know how we're going to be able to get it to the gas station in time."

"I'll check on it," Bob says.

Bob goes out to the barn and checks the Buick. He climbs inside, turns on the ignition, and looks at the gas gauge to see if it has gas.

"It's all taken care of, Dad," Bob says when he returns. "The car is back, and it's got gas."

"Oh good," my father says. He is calmed by this news. He closes his eyes and sleeps.

In the morning, Bob is going to work for a few hours and I am to stay home with Daddy-o. It takes Bob some time to go. The car is dead—not because it doesn't have gas, but because Bob left the lights on last night when he checked. After AAA arrives and jumps the car, we move Dad back to the hospital bed we've set up in the Pine Room so that he will have a fine day watching the sky and the horses in the field. We open the glass doors so it will be like he is outside with the birds. Very shortly after Bob finally leaves, the hospice nurse arrives. I leave her with Pop and sit in the other room.

A minute later, she comes in and sits next to me.

"Your father's blood pressure is seventy over nothing," she whispers. "So it will be very soon. I cannot tell you how soon, but I'd say anytime. Someone needs to talk to him about signing over to hospice and the DNR."

Susan the Nurse is tall and pretty and talks with a thick Boston accent. I look at her and my breath catches. *How do we do this?* I think. *How do you tell a man he is dying?* Again.

We move into the other room, and I hold my father as Susan the Nurse tells him things. "Mr. Montgomery, do you understand what's happening? Mr. Montgomery, do you understand you are not getting better?" I hold on for dear life and watch my father's face stand still. I don't know if he understands, but he nods.

"Dad, are you with us?" I ask.

He looks at me, stoned, but nods.

"Dad," I squeeze his hand. "Dad," I repeat.

"Dad, you're not getting any better. You know that. You know that this is it. We are moving to another place right now. Unless an angel comes down right now and cures you, you will not be getting better. We want to shift you over to hospice now because we don't want to have to call 911. We don't want them to come and drag you back. We want you to be able to go peacefully."

Susan the Nurse helps me, as does Marie, Dad's health care worker, his Haitian princess. I hold onto him on one side and Marie holds onto the other, and we tell him what will happen.

Mother hobbles in and takes his hand. "Monty," she says. He turns and looks at her with the widest smile. "It's time to go to the great big cocktail party in the sky," she says. "I've always loved you."

I know Pops is out of it because he just smiles as if she's talking about the weather. She begins to cry and leaves the room.

"Are you afraid, Dad?" I ask. "Do you want to know what's going to be happening?"

He nods.

"You will quietly slip away," Susan says. "There will be nothing violent. Your systems will simply shut down and you will stop breathing. It will be like going to sleep. You won't be awake, your spirit will move on."

"Whatever is happening right now we cannot change," I say. "We need to ask for help. You need to be able to ask for help. All you have to do is say 'Help' in your head. 'Help.'"

And that's how it is. The nurse, the Haitian princess, and I talk to my father and tell him about faith. About asking for help. Letting go. My father is not a religious man, but nevertheless I persevere with stories of the other side. I tell him that it's a good place, even though I don't know that.

"Are you afraid?"

My father is very afraid. I can see the fear in his eyes. I tell him about a book I read about God: *God: The Evidence.* "It was written, Dad, it was written by a member of your favorite party. The Grand Old Party. Those assholes, Dad, a Reagan cabinet member, a foreign policy expert. He reviewed everything there is . . . and you know what, there is just enough evidence of a higher order of things, maybe not God-God, but something. We have to trust, now. We have no choice."

At that moment, my father issues his last words when we again ask him about the DNR.

"I don't know," he says. "Let my family decide."

The hospice nurse gives us instructions to increase the anxiety and pain medicine, and when we do he says he wants to return to his bedroom. We all manage to get him in the wheelchair and take him to his bedroom and his own bed. He quickly slips away into never-never land, unable to wake. I lie with him then, and we breathe. His chest rises and falls. His eyes are half open, his jaw is slack, and the sounds of air traveling back and forth are hollow.

Later, Bob returns, checks in, and then disappears. When I look for him, I run upstairs on the carpet of tiny green, red, and yellow stripes and remember the last time my father took these stairs. It was March, and he did so slowly, painstakingly. Each step was a triumph, his hand gripping the rail. Going down was different—he cruised down quickly as I yelled, *Be careful!*

"Bob," I call.

"Yep." I follow his voice and find him lying in the room that was my bedroom as a child. He lies in a bed known as a hired-man's bed. It is small and wooden and hard. He holds his hands across his chest like my father, and his feet, as wide and strange as Dad's, cross at the ankles, his toes wiggling together as if trying to reassure themselves. His feet are my father's feet, the very same. They wiggle in the same way.

"Hi," I say.

"Hi," he says, but he does not turn to face me.

He moves slightly; some part of his body shifts, a shoulder that shows his discomfort.

"I'm pretending I'm Dad." He pushes his folded hands in the air to indicate that he is doing this hand business, the way my father crosses his hands over his chest when he sleeps.

"Do you sleep that way?"

He smirks.

"I don't know."

He looks out the window. It must be early evening, naptime. We are tired and sad. I move my eyes to where my brother stares and find a roof that wasn't here when I was a child but was added as part of an addition after I left. Otherwise the view here is the same and I remember being very small and convincing myself that I saw Santa Claus and all of his reindeer darting across the sky. In my memory at least, back then it snowed reliably in December in New England, sometimes even, magically, on Christmas Eve.

In the other wall, at the front of the house, are two windows. The telephone wires and poles and streetlight visible there are all burned into the landscape of my subconscious, as are the sounds of the night, my father getting up and using the bathroom, then his footsteps in the morning, the jingle of the lock that kept me inside my room when I was small because I liked to wander at two in the morning to play in Lael's jewelry box and steal Bob's clothes.

"Time to get up," my father would call.

"This sucks," I finally say to my brother.

"Yep," he says but offers nothing else except for this vision here—hands and fingers and ankles crossed, and those toes wiggling so preciously.

I turn and walk out of the room, down the hall, down the stairs, through the dining room and kitchen, and into my parents' bedroom, where I find Marie, the Haitian princess, sitting by my father's side, holding his hand watching his face as he breathes. I climb into bed and hold the other hand, and we breathe together. In. Out. Hollow sounds. She focuses so intently on my father's face, I imagine she is trying to will him to another plane. Not me. Despite a blood pressure of seventy over nothing, I stubbornly think that something else is going on. We gave him too much lorazepam. That and the morphine. I tell myself the man is drugged, not dying.

Even here at the end of the road, as I imagine my father moving like a wind, picking up last-minute items and unhooking weights as if untethering a hot air balloon, I see myself running behind him and, with every breath, I carefully hook them back onto him. I hold his hands. I rub his feet, trying to push the blood through him. His body is cold and growing blue. I study the ceiling and then again the windows that overlook the front of the house. They are small windows located at the top of a wall in order to let air and light in, but they afford no view. The view comes from the other side of the room. All those days I watched my father stare at these windows, believing that there was something there to capture his attention—a bird or piece of sky—there was nothing but the reflection of his life, the great weight of all those years to let go. For hours over the last months, as I watched him stare, he was busy, preparing for the enormous task of unbuttoning all the buttons, unhooking all the connections and obligations that kept him here.

When the hospice nurse returns, my mother and brother sign all the hospice papers on the kitchen table. My mother is so gone on sadness and gin that she will not remember signing the papers, and the next morning I will watch her face run cold when she sees her signature on every dotted line, but during that afternoon, after all the "Do Not Resuscitate" paperwork is added to Bob's notebook, he begins the weary chore of calling around about funeral homes—who's good, who's not. In California, Lael and her husband Jon, having returned home just the evening before, pack and ready themselves to climb back on a plane the following morning at, it turns out, almost the same minute my father will take his last breath.

But now it is early evening. I lie next to my father, who stares at the small paned windows. The Haitian princess prepares to go home. We still have many hours to go.

I lean over and place a hand on his shoulder. "Dad," I say.

It is six o'clock and time for his medication, but I cannot wake him. I try again, shaking him a little. His eyes are half open, cloudy and blue. It is an eerie sight, my father's face, silent, frozen, the only sound this incessant wind blowing through him.

I can't wake him up. Bob tries. Mother tries. As Stoyan might say, he is not happening.

Popalicious is in nowheresville.

I pull out the hospice pamphlet and reread all the signs that death is imminent, whispering to my brother as we sit in the kitchen. Breathing. Congestion. Restlessness. Eyes half open.

Generally, I continue reading, *a person becomes nonresponsive.*

Bob looks annoyed, so I read on silently.

How we approach death is going to depend upon our fear of life, how much we participated in that life, and how willing we are to let go of this known expression to venture into a new one. Fear and unfinished business are two big factors in determining how much resistance we put into meeting death.

The separation becomes complete when breathing stops. What appears to be the last breath is often followed by one or two long spaced breaths and then the physical body is empty. The owner is no longer in need of a heavy, nonfunctioning vehicle.

They have entered a new city, a new life.

I place the little blue pamphlet with the ship on the cover under the jars of vitamins my father refused to take. Outside the windows, there are no birds at the feeder, but beyond, in the clouds in the sky, I imagine a city far away, nestled in mountains of white air, and I picture my father from behind as he prepares for the long journey ahead.

I guess it's time for you to fly, Pops, I think. *Time to fly, old man.*

In my heart, I imagine death's beginning: Smoke and fireflies, a butter lamp sputters. There are the girls in pink with their daisies from the field. His blood slows, his heart turns in on itself; whispers, drips. *How does he keep breathing? Dad? Are you breathing? Bob? Is he breathing?*

I close my eyes and try to imagine where he is and what he is seeing. At first, I see only darkness. Then, there are a few shifts of color and shards of spilled light, the smell of the lake from the center of his father's boat, the Black Bomber. He turns the wheel and water moves effortlessly around the hull, spraying out the sides like small round wings. He pushes the accelerator forward and bombs along the lake's rocky edge. His hair feels delicious, flying in the wind. He knows the boulders of this lake by heart. Summer after summer, he has studied each cove, each island. He now darts between them expertly, the boat bursting into circles, triumphant, faster and faster, around and around. He tightens his fingers around the steering wheel of the boat. Down the lake there is the girl he will marry. How can life be over? It's summer, and he's falling in love.

16

NIGHT

June 7, 1999
Framingham, Massachusetts

Bob sleeps on the floor in my parents' room. I sleep on a couch two rooms over. As the clock moves into the small dark hours, we wake and go to our father, hold on to him.

He is unconscious. Since we only have morphine in tablets and he cannot swallow, we have no way to give him his pain medicine. We wait for the pharmacy to deliver his liquid morphine, but the pharmacy does not come. I try to figure out the drug's concentrations when we split pills.

If you put ten milligrams in ten milliliters, you have one milligram per milliliter. Bob and I begin calculating doses of morphine on paper napkins. We have no syringes to measure with, only teaspoons.

"Ten milliliters is a lot to administer. How 'bout five?"

There is no time release when the pills are broken up.

At seven that evening I call the hospice nurse to let her know that Dad is unconscious, and we have no way to deliver any medicine to him. The pharmacy was supposed to deliver everything by seven. She tells me she will check on it and call me back.

"It's on its way," she says.

At eight o'clock, there is still no word, so I call again and I am told the same thing. At nine o'clock there is still no word, so I call again and am told the same thing. *And on and on.*

Ten. Eleven. At midnight we learn that the medicine is not coming because The Oncologist didn't call in the prescription.

Bob and I begin grinding more morphine in a pretty china eggcup, mixing ground up tranquilizers and morphine into ice cream, and dripping the mixture into the well between my father's bottom lip and lower teeth.

"Dad, swallow."

"Swallow! Swallow!"

"Did he swallow?"

"Bob, don't let him choke."

"He's not choking."

"He got it."

"No, he chewed it."

"Oh no!"

"Yes, he swallowed. Yes."

"He did? He didn't."

"He's got it."

"He doesn't."

This is hell.

We try again.

My father does not wake up until one A.M. When he does, he is screaming, and writhing in pain. He is terrified.

He is dying. He points to a corner in the room. He is see-ing things that we cannot see. I hold his hands. He cannot speak, but he is wide awake. "Dad. It's okay. Dad. Breathe." He gestures with his fingers over and over on his face, point-ing to his temple. I kiss him. I kiss his face, and he closes his eyes.

Bob comes in and sees Dad calmer. "The medicine is beginning to work," he says. "The nurse is on her way."

She arrives about an hour later, apologizing about the liquid morphine, and, rolling Dad over, begins stuffing mor-phine tablets up his ass.

When morning comes, I go outside to wander the backyard and the field, to water the flowers and this year's garden that is hardly planted. There are blueberries. The peonies are blooming; the asparagus is still making a great show. The strawberries are here, and the daisies are spectacular. The sun moves up the wall of the barn, and there are fat breasted robins and blue jays. I water the petunias that Lael planted along the pathways. I water the whiskey barrels with their perfectly bored holes, and I return to Dad. I hold his hands and tell him a flood of things: how he is the best father, how I will remember him in every berry on the planet, in daisies and dahlias, zinnias and bales of hay. I tell him how I love him, what a good, decent man he is, and as hard as it has been, that I understand his decisions, the way he patiently, painstakingly forgave my head-in-the-clouds ways, the way, yes, in which he stuck by my mother, not because it was or would be my decision but because it was his decision and his life; he tried to do the right and solid thing. I tell him how grateful I am for this time over the months when I began to know him and to inhabit myself.

"The gardens are watered," I finally say. "Lael, Jon, and Tom are on their way. Bob, Mom, and I are here. We will take care of Mother. We are fine, Dad. Everything is ready. It's time for you to go. It's okay for you to go."

I climb into bed, and, holding his hand watch him breathe, and think about a dream I had only a week before, when Tom and I were staying on the river:

My father was in a blue room. He lay in a hospital bed and stared at the ceiling, smirking. It was a room I did not know, but it was somehow familiar. It was square and had windows on every wall. I looked into my father's eyes. They were his eyes, hazel, small, and squinting. In the corners, tears popped out in crystals, brilliant translucent stones. "I have seen so many miracles," he said, half smiling. He stood and walked. We were planning on going to the doctor. He did not say this but it was understood. He was all bones, but strong. His pelvis was a wide disk, his bottom droopy with skin.

I will never forget his frozen feet in the days before he died. In the dream, his bare feet slip-slipped as they shuffled; my father's wide feet with weird toes like mine. When his circulation begins to shut off, his feet turn blue like icicles. I rub them trying to coax blood into them and I can't help but notice his hands again—how they have not changed. Feeling my own hands, I think about how my fingers get cold and numb when I sleep. As I watch my father die that morning, this is what I think about: I realize how I am like him in this way, how I too cross my hands over my chest when I sleep.

17

ENDS

Tuesday
June 8, 1999

This is how my father takes his last breath: Unlike in the movies, it is not a grand gesture. It is an infinitely small thing. He swallows air. His mouth reaches toward the sky as if he is a fish out of water. His throat makes a small clicking sound. It is 10:04 A.M. Eastern Standard Time and in that moment—two breaths reaching, swallowing—I watch my father's life end. A wisp of nothing circles to the sky, expands and contracts; it turns in the wind, makes a sound like the snap of a sail. The man of ghostly sticks breaks apart, drifts away. In an instant, his life becomes something else, something complete in its end, a circle that bends and twists, a helix through time. I turn him around in my heart. I see him in the palm of my hand. I see him from many sides, all the nooks and crannies, the soft underbelly of a life visible now in its absence.

My brother sits in a chair next to the bed, where I lie on

the other side of my father. Both of us hold his hands and cry as he dies, both of us having told him in those last moments, as we had over the last hours and days and months, how much we love him. My brother says, *I love you, Dad,* and these words, his voice, run around my mind over and over and over for months. I watch confusion spread across my brother's face as he realizes Dad is no longer breathing.

"Is he . . . ?"

I nod.

We sit incredulous, still. We hold onto our father; we wait to see if he will breathe. I study my father's white face. After a while, Bob's fingers reach up to close the lids over his eyes, and I wonder how he knew to do that. Had he seen the same television shows as I?

Bob stands. I crawl off the bed, holding onto my father's feet, and my brother and I hold onto each other, our bodies heaving. I run out to tell Mother, who is sitting with Stoyan in the pine room, and they follow me back to the bedroom. My mother hobbles in and cries. Stoyan plucks two daisies from a nearby vase and places one in each of my father's ears, then picks up his clarinet and wanders the house playing *When the Saints Come Marching In.* Mother asks if someone can please close Dad's mouth. Bob reaches to my father's jaw and it is solid, frozen open. I see my father's Adam's apple quiet as a stone and remember pushing it as a child, fascinated with that hard knot in his throat beneath a birthmark shaped like a heart. *Do it again!* My father swallows and I watch the heart-shaped thing in his throat wiggle. *Again! An apple in a throat. An apple in my father's throat!*

You were just a tadpole, then, I hear him say.

I see my father alive. He looks up at me from his bed.

Shit, I say. *I think I left the bath running.*

Oh, no, he smiles, shakes his head as if to say, *Kid, you are incorrigible.*

I point a finger to the air. "I'll be back," I tell him and I turn, running through the kitchen, the dining room, and up the stairs, two at a time, to the bath. It is empty. I had imagined it. I run back down the stairs, returning to my father.

Well?

No, I imagined it.

Smiling: *Do you remember the night when you feel asleep in the bath?*

No. I sit next to him on the bed. He puts his hand out and fiddles with the rings on my left hand. *Pretty,* he says.

You fell asleep. You did. We couldn't find you anywhere and when I checked the bath, you were there, floating sound asleep. Scared me half to death.

He smiles again. *You were just a tadpole then.*

You know there was a time I carried you up to bed every night. You would fall asleep on the couch and I carried you up and then one time I went on a business trip and you never let me do it again.

Did I say why?

No, but you were mad.

I'm sorry, Dad.

I never understood it.

He fiddles with my bracelets. He pinches me to see if I'm still alive and then he giggles when I yell, "Ouch!"

We look out over the field. Standing by the bed, I bend down and lay my head next to his body and I can remember what it felt like when he stroked my hair and I do not want to move, feeling his hand stroke my hair. I want it never to end.

Later that morning after my father dies, I get on the phone to the hospice nurse. I call the hospice pharmacy. I call The Oncologist's nurse. I call The Oncologist's secretary.

I don't understand, I tell the nurse and then, the pharmacy.

They tell me: The doctor did not call in the prescription. The pharmacy did not call the nurse to tell her the doctor hadn't called.

Why not? I ask the pharmacy and the nurse. Why not? I ask The Oncologist and his secretary. I don't understand. After a night of hell, of calling every hour on the hour, the hospice nurse putting morphine tablets in my father's rectum at two in the morning, my father dying, my brother and I out of our minds with horror, my brother trying to hold everything together, trying to do right by my father, trying to keep me asleep so I won't yell at him for chopping up too much morphine.

"Why not?" I ask.

"We didn't think it was an emergency," the secretary finally says.

"I'm sorry," one of the oncology nurses tells me later.

"Sorry for who?" I ask. "The person you should feel sorry for is dead."

There is a hush across the house, an exhaustion. It is a hot, sunny morning. I walk in circles through all the rooms, again and again. As I do, I am steeped in years of summers here: slamming of porch doors, the making of sandwiches after a morning of chores and grocery shopping, the thump and whine of the fridge door, the sound of ice crunching in my father's teeth.

On the table, I find the notebook we have used to keep track of Pop's final weeks. Bob has written the last page in perfect handwriting:

9–11 Could not get Dad to swallow meds and liquid ones had not arrived. Pharmacy claims it never got the prescription from doctor.

1. Woke up. Eyes wide. Scared and under a lot of pain. Gave him first 10 ml of Roxicodone, lorazepam and 15 mg of MS Contin (split) in ice-cream.

1:15 Then a whole 15mg MS Contin which he may have chewed. Spoke to hospice nurse and she suggested I put lorazepam under his tongue, which I did. Started to take effect at 1:50.

2:00 Nurse (Rose) came took vital signs and blood pressure (70/48.) She gave him 30 mg MS Contin rectally.

2:45 Dad well sedated. Nurse left oral syringe for giving dis-solved lorazepam or liquid Roxicodone.

5:30 A.M. Dad woke with a lot of pain, administered 10 ml of Roxicodone, 2 lorazepan (dissolved) and 30 mg of MS Contin (dissolved.) At 6 A.M., he was sedated.

8:15 Dad started to get restless, eyes open—administered 2 dissolved lorazepam. Respiration 18 min, Pulse 47 minute.

8:40 Pain was returning; lips exposing upper teeth, moaning. Administered 30 mg MS Contin dissolved.

8:50 Liquid.

9:45 Couldn't find pulse; respiration at 18. Nurse Susan arrived. Susan couldn't get blood pressure. Respiration 16/min. Temp 95. Susan says stay @ 30 mg/3 hour (.6 ml/3 hr liquid morphine).

10:05 Dad died quietly.

18

FIREFLIES

Tuesday, June 8
Framingham, Massachusetts

For a short time after my father dies, I sit with him and touch his bones, putting my hands on his cold feet, up the tibia and the knee, the big leg bone, the hip, one side of his ribs, the bones of the chest, shoulders, an elbow, fingers. I pull back his pajamas and trace a finger along the scar on his chest and place the palm of my hand over the contraption with which they infused chemo, and then put both my hands onto his still chest.

When there is a knock on the front door, I leave my father's corpse to find the pharmacy man standing on the front steps. His car is parked at the front of the house, on the side of the road. He holds out a white bag.

"Too late. He's dead."

Nothing on the man moves but an eyebrow, as if a tiny string pulls a muscle in his brow. He stands for a long time looking at me, holding out the bag.

"I have to deliver it," he says.

"He's dead," I say. "We don't need it anymore."

"I have to deliver it."

"We don't need it," I whisper. "He's dead."

We stand looking at one another, and after that, I don't remember what happens. Bob tells me I never went to the door, that he went to the door, but that's not what I remember. I remember going to the door and seeing the man and his white sedan, and saying those things and thinking how ironic it was that this poor man was delivering medicine for my dead father. I think I carried the medicine into the house with me and then the nurse became involved, and then Bob became involved, and the man—still standing at the door—took the liquid morphine back.

❦

Later, my brother sits by father's corpse, his bony body now rock hard in his blue and white pinstriped pajamas, his lips white, his face empty, frozen into the lifeless mask he had been wearing for days. Bob turns to me.

"How 'bout we take Dad to the funeral home in the MG," he says. "We can put a hat and glasses on him and take him for a last ride."

"I don't know, Bob," I say.

"Oh, no," Mother says. She sits on the ledge of her buggy on her side of the bed, stares at Pop, gets up, wheels around to the foot of the bed, and sits again.

"He'd like it," he says.

"I know you're right," I say. "I just don't know."

"Maybe I should go," Mother says. "I don't want you to be arrested. If I'm arrested, it won't matter."

"Nah, I don't think so," I say now staring into my father's closet, counting Topsiders, he had many pairs, and I think how these things are meaningless now—just a dead man's things.

∞

The sun comes through the window for an instant, then disappears.

The funeral home man comes to retrieve my father's corpse. He is a small man with a glass eye who speaks in the smooth undertones considered appropriate for such occasions.

"We know this is a difficult time," he says. *Hushbuzz. Hushbuzz.* We all assemble around what was our father. The short man, his glass eye slightly askew, is followed by a tall man who is introduced as Shorty.

"You couldn't possibly be serious," I say.

"No," the short man insists. "This is Shorty."

Shorty takes my father's shoulders, the short man takes his feet, and they lift him onto the black gurney and zip up the body bag. They wheel him out into the hallway, and then out the door, where they lose their footing and my father's corpse, stiff like *papier-mâché,* begins to slide into the procession of impatiens planted by Lael according to my father's instructions. Bob jumps. My hand moves to cover my mouth in horror as the short funeral home man and the man named Shorty catch my father's body before it hits the ground. Then Bob and I begin to laugh. *Oh my God! It's not funny!*

Once his body is gone, Mother climbs into bed. Bob, Sue, and I sit by the pool drinking wine. We're all exhausted, but Bob and I want to mark this time by doing something Dad loved. So, we get up and crawl into the MG TD and cruise all the back country roads.

They burn my father's body with a daisy in his ear.

"Did they burn Daddy yet?" my mother asks. It is the day after my father died and we are eating a ham salad brought by a neighbor.

"Thursday," Bob says, his mouth full.

When the short man returns with my father's ashes a day later, they are in a box, gift wrapped with a gold seal. I pick them up and shake. They are heavier than I expected. I remember my Granny Montgomery's ashes seemed heavy, too. A few years before, on the rainy November day of her funeral, my father and I retrieved them at the little house at the Ayre cemetery. They were in a tan, plastic box with specks of color in it. Dad and I opened the little rubber top to take a peek.

"Wow, there are pieces of bone," I said.

"Really?" My father took the box and, closing one eye, peered inside with the other. "How 'bout that?" We looked at one another uncomfortably. *Poor Granny,* we said. *Poor Mother.*

I place Dad's ashes along with his glasses and hat on the bed next to my mother. His glasses are still dirty with his oils, his scent. Later, Mother walks around with my gift-wrapped father from the crematorium perched precariously on the basket of her purple racing walker, her gin martini on the ledge above the basket, and as she pushes the walker over the threshold of the room, the box holding my father falls to the ground, followed by the martini. Horrified, Bob scoops up the box and runs it upstairs to the office for safe-keeping.

"Where is your father," Mother asks later.

"I don't know," I say. I look around and put my hands out, palms to the sky like a holy person. "He could be any-where. Everywhere?"

Outside Bob plays his tuba wearing brown cotton gloves. I watch out the window as Mother sits in front of him. She is so sad. She sits in front of my brother on the deck over-looking a pool and the field, where Dad's whiskey barrels are full of flowers, tomatoes, and basil, and listens to Bob mak-ing hollow farting sounds on his tuba. Mother is glaring, and though I want to help her, I know he has saved our father from a terrible end.

"I don't want to be vacuuming up Dad," Bob says. "That would be too . . . you know . . ."

"No, that would not be a good thing," I say.

"Though if it did happen," Bob adds. "We could always use a new vacuum cleaner bag."

My family is full of such dislocated passion. We wander, not knowing how to deal with ourselves or each other or this sadness about Big Dad. We sit here with our broken hearts as my brother makes these silly sounds, *Oompah-pah, Oompah-pah,* moving his head just so, here and there, left and right, and I feel like we might be in a circus.

"Where is your father?" Mother says again.

"Down cellar behind the ax," I hear my father yell.

"I want your father," she says. "You have no right," to which no one says anything. The only sounds waft from my brother's tuba in up and down notes.

I turn away and look out at the field and think, *Shit, it's already summer.*

∞

We have so many things to do and are full of so many questions. *Obituaries and memorials. Now what? What newspapers do we send the obituary to? What town did his father's family live in? What picture? What society did he belong to in Worcester? Who do we invite? Where should donations go? Do you remember all his photographs of flowers?*

We want to assemble something special for the memory of Big Dad. In the end, we plan a small backyard memorial brunch with a three-piece Bulgarian jazz band led by Stoyan on clarinet. Stoyan's friend, Daddy Long Legs, is on piano, and I don't remember the third guy. There is a ballet in the field, performed and choreographed by my father's little friend, Kaitlin, whose pony lives in our barn. We hire a caterer who sets up umbrellas and tables and a huge buffet with a full open bar. Mother wears her fishnet stockings and a black Bolero hat reminiscent of the one Bo Derek wore in the movie *Ten.*

When the music begins and the girl dances a sad dance waving a transparent blue scarf, Mother sits quickly and grabs her vase of gin. A handful of fresh mint and two red-and-white striped straws, lipstick smudged on the ends, poke out the top. Directly behind me, I hear someone whisper.

"Who is the babe in the stockings?"

"The widow," my husband Tom whispers back.

I begin to laugh and turn around to see Tom and his brother laughing too.

I turn back toward my mother and see she is now holding hands with her psychiatrist, a man whose moon face is reminiscent of Truman Capote's, and I can hear my father chuckle at the sight. I know he would have been amused.

"You gottabekiddinme." Tom's brother says.

"No shit. That's Barb, my mother-in-law."

Behind us is that tinny turquoise of the backyard swimming pool and beyond that the tiny, star-like flowers of fuchsia impatiens. Next to the garden is a pool house and dotted all around are the festive umbrellas of the caterer's tables. As the dance continues, I turn to the back field and, seeing the miles of waist-high daisies, remember that this is my father's favorite time of the year. Planting time, with spring sprung and four glorious growing months ahead.

Earlier that morning, I set up an altar full of sprigs from his garden, his favorite cigarettes, a glass of beer, and photographs of him throughout his life. We don't invite many people and plan no service because we have no idea of what Mother will be up to. After the dance, I read a poem called *He's Not Dead, Just Away.* As I do, Mother gets up and wheels back into the house with her entourage. She tells me later she couldn't handle it without bursting. It doesn't matter. I am determined to continue. Afterward, when my dad's business partners tell funny stories about him, I recognize my father's precise brand of story telling in these men, the way they rock on their heels, jingle the change in their pockets, and laugh at the same moments as if in harmony.

When the party winds down, I bring the men to my father's garden and, just inside the barn, his workshop, where

I show them the things I know he loved—the *doohickeys, yahoos, thingamajigs,* and other marvels he engineered in his garden to keep the vegetables and fruits safe from critters. His friends poke through the collection of contraptions— the *melon keeper-uppers* and *rabbit keeper-outers* and the plastic runner that made the squirrels slip off the ropes so they couldn't pig the bird food. They shake their heads at Pop's antics and ingenuity.

"Only fucking Montgomery would think of PCV tubing to roll squirrels," one of the men says, shaking his head. They all laugh.

I laugh, too. Enveloped by the smell of the earth, and the sweet meld of horse and fresh hay, I walk to the back of the room to open the barn doors. A hot summer wind moves up from the field. It seems impossible, unbelievable that my father is dead, and as I look into the faces of his friends whom I've known since I was a child, I am not at all sure about how I will go on. As long as my father's feet were firmly on the ground, I could carry on, but without him, it feels like there is no more earth, nor bone nor skin, to hold me.

As it grows dark, the sadness of these months lingers in the hot air, but I realize that it is a beautiful, unifying sadness. As fractured and lonely as our family has been, we were able to come together, however briefly, again. That night, Bob and Susan drive home to their own house and the rest of us— Mother, Lael, Jon, Tom, and I—move into our rooms at the back of the house to sleep and to think about it all. *Did we do okay by him? Did we do the best we could? Is he in a better place?*

I lie in bed staring at the ceiling and think of my mother, alone now after sixty years of falling in and out of love, and try to imagine the depth of her sorrow. I grasp at my own and think, *Like this, only bigger?*

"Hey, Lee," I hear from outside the window. "Lee."

I get up and go to the window and see Tom sitting below, having a smoke.

"Look!" he says. He switches the porch light off and in the field is a sea of tiny pulsing lights. Everywhere I look, I see billions of blinking lights.

"Fireflies," Tom says.

"Hey, Lael," I yell, running to knock on her door.

"What?" she yells back.

"Look outside," I say through the door. "Stealth Dad."

I return to the window, rest my elbows on the sill, and hang outside.

A second later Lael's head pops out. "Wow!" she says.

We're both silent then, watching the show of lights and I cannot help but think about how Dad would have relished this sight. I imagine him at the bottom of the field, turning back one more time before he disappears, and there inside his house, visible in the windows, are the bobbing heads of his two astonished daughters, blinking.

"Wow!" Lael says, "Can you believe it?"

I watch the light for a long time and when I turn away I hear myself say, "Would you look at that? They sure are pretty."

Only a moment passes before I realize the words are his. And I want to believe, like I believed there was magic in the games Dad and I played in my childhood—the stolen noses and disappearing pennies—that this means he remains with us. The millions of blinking lights might be his finale of sorts, a final wink, his way of showing us there's more to this life than we will ever know. I don't know how else to think about it. I've known this house all my life, and never have seen that field aglow, before or since, never so full, never so bright.

ACKNOWLEDGMENTS

I owe my greatest thanks to my family. I am indebted to my love—my friend and husband—Thomas, for everything, beginning with our long walks in Paris. I am grateful for the love of his parents, Tom and Theresa, and the friendship, love, and support of my sibs, Lael and Bob. Without them, there would be no story because none of this would have been survivable.

I am especially indebted to my spirit guides Barbara Shore and Deidra Walpole and the early, early encouragement of Susan Montgomery, who always liked my letters.

I am grateful for the friendship and guidance from my mentor Jim Krusoe, who first taught me about story, the beauty of the path not taken, and the word not used. Thanks also to Jenny Krusoe and their son, godson Henry James, who waits most patiently for instructions.

Early on there were friends and readers who believed in this project long before anyone else. Without the support of Eric Walsh, Elaine Ettinger, Connie Wright, Mary Colvig, Angela Fasick, Michelle Latiolais, Melany Runyan, Andrew Tonkovich, Anna Keesey, Ellen Fagg, Margot Meyers, and

Jennifer Whitcomb, I would have most certainly jumped off a bridge.

I am indebted to the Brick House Literary Agency and particularly Judy Heiblum for her steady orienteering, unflappable critiques, and wisdom. I am grateful to editor extraordinaire Wylie O'Sullivan for her life experience, sense of adventure, keen eye, and expertise. Thank you to Martha Levin and Dominick Anfuso for venturing forward with the project and coming uptown for a martini and party.

I am beholden to all the wonderful folks at Tin House with special thanks to Holly MacArthur and Win (*What Book?*) McCormack for their friendship. I would also like to thank CJ Evans, Meg Storey, and Emily Bliquez for their patience and encouragement, and Laura Shaw for her art saves.

I am indebted to the mighty Columbia River and all the friends of the wind.

I am grateful for the support of the Caldera residency and the Barber Fellowship at Squaw Valley Community of Writers.

Finally, life would be unbearable without Greentool, the stinkies, and all those wonderful folks in the chapel at the Inn of the Seventh Ray in Ah, Topanga Canyon, who inspired this great journey, and those in the studio on Kearney who keep me there.

ABOUT THE AUTHOR

LEE MONTGOMERY is the editorial director of Tin House Books and the executive editor for *Tin House* magazine. She was the founding and executive director for the Tin House summer writers workshop. She has edited numerous books, literary journals, and anthologies including *The Iowa Review, Santa Monica Review, Transgressions: The Iowa Anthology of Innovative Fiction* and *Absolute Disaster: Fiction from LA*. Her stories and nonfiction have appeared in publications such as the *Black Clock, Alaska Quarterly, The Iowa Review, Denver Quarterly, Story Magazine, Travel Holiday, The Hollywood Reporter,* and *Santa Monica Review.* She lives in Portland, Oregon.

THE
THINGS BETWEEN US

A Memoir

Lee Montgomery

A Conversation with Lee Montgomery

Reading Group Guide

ABOUT THIS GUIDE

The following author interview and reading group guide are intended to help you find interesting and rewarding approaches to your reading of *The Things Between Us*. We hope these elements enhance your enjoyment and appreciation of the book.

A CONVERSATION WITH
LEE MONTGOMERY

BY DAVE WEICH

Was your childhood at all typical among your peers in Framingham?

In that area, there was a pocket full of fancy people. In the late 1800s and early 1900s people who lived on Beacon Hill had their country estates in Framingham. And though, over time, they were sold and parceled off, many of them stayed the same. The types of families that gravitated to that area evolved from those beginnings. The social register was important to them. People went to debutante parties, if they were chosen. We all went to private schools. We rode in hunt clubs. My mother and a group of other people founded what was "a country club" for the masses, the Belknap Pool. At the time, she had big fights with some people because they didn't want black people there, and they didn't want Jewish people.

This would have been the sixties?

Yes, they moved to that house in the fifties. A lot of that old world stuff still existed.

The present frame of *The Things between Us* concludes in 1999, seven years ago. How did time and distance help you process these events and turn them into a book?

The book started as an essay. I was encouraged by a workshop at Squaw Valley; some people thought I should make it a book. I wrote the original draft quickly, in about six months, a narrative about my father. It was as if I needed to put it down because I wanted to freeze the time. I wanted to remember everything about it. I wanted to remember everything about *him*.

I sent it out and found some interest, but it was still half-baked. I worked with a couple different agents who had some ideas about revisions. I developed two separate sets of revisions, but it just wasn't there. It was *their* idea of what it should be. So I put it aside. I walked around for a couple years, thinking, *I just don't know what this book is about.*

I remember there was one person in New York who said, "You can't sell the book because it's about dying. It's all about death." And I said, "Well, it's a book about death." And that was before September 11. Anyway, I put it away.

A few years later I tried one more revision. I tried fictionalizing it. I included a lot of sections about my mother. I added photographs and blacked out the eyes. I really just had a blast tearing the whole thing apart. Part of it appeared in the *Santa Monica Review*. The book wasn't working, so I was just going to publish the essay and call it good.

When I published the essay, an agent saw it and asked to see the book. I sent her the original memoir, the second draft. She liked it and asked for a couple revisions, so I included a lot of the autobiographical stuff I had written about my mother in the novel; I started folding in the narrative of my mother and my family. Eventually it all came together.

You wrote, "I will never be able to explain my mother, but I will most likely spend my life trying."

The book's out now. Granted you're just beginning to deal with public reaction, but do you feel any closer to explaining?

Yes, in that there is no explanation, there is no way to resolve it, there is no happy ending. She said she was sorry years ago, and I accept that. She didn't mean to be a drunk. I don't think people set out to do that. I suppose the book was helpful in letting me grieve, and accepting and forgiving both of them for the choices they made.

In early reviews, people have written at length about your mother. I'm not surprised to hear that she wasn't part of the original draft. The book's not about her. She's central, though, and without question she brings a whole lot of color. As the book was transforming from a story about your father to a larger family history, did you feel that your mother was hijacking it?

Definitely. But it's so typical. She hijacks everything. That's always been my experience. She hijacked the cover. She hijacked the story. She's a showstopper. I think maybe that's what people mention in reviews because it is the most colorful part. The relationship between my father and me was more settled, and a lot sadder. Mother is a sad story, but she was so flamboyant. I think people gravitate to that levity and color. She's so unbelievable. People say, "I love that cover," and I think, *She's a showstopper, that one.*

That was the reason I didn't include her when I first tried writing the book. Mother had hijacked my fiction; she'd always done that. I have notebooks of stuff about my mom that I've written over the years. I wanted to make this separate.

If anything has happened, at least that's settled. I'm done. I don't think I have to write about it again, and I'm very happy about that. A lot of my stories, and the novel that is in a basket at home, include this territory, this landscape. Class, drunks.

There's a line in the book, "This dying business is about endings, yes, but also quite possibly its difficulty carves a tiny space in people's hearts for something new." How did your father's fight with cancer change you?

Death is a great advisor, and I'm not the first person to say that. When you look at life through death, that lens, it's much more precious. Trespasses are much more forgivable. You're able to appreciate the things that *did* go right, in my case the lovely things about our family and my parents. It provided perspective.

When I looked at my father at the end of his life and considered my own immortality, all of a sudden the fact that he wouldn't let me go out with what's-his-face, or whatever, all those things fell away. A lot of the sadness fell away. It was just gratitude.

It's not unlike the way you look at life when you're writing fiction: everything is frozen and held up to appreciate, to look at again. Everything is slowed down to a stop, the way it is when you're describing a scene or a landscape.

It completely blew my mind, watching my father take his last breath. It's a lot like birth, that whole process. For people that die of natural causes, there's a labor. It's otherworldly. I don't know that it made me believe in God, but I thought, *This is much bigger than I will ever be able to understand.*

What traits did you inherit from your father?

I look like him. I've got knees like him, unfortunately. I wish I had legs like my mother. And I'm not practical, that's for sure. He couldn't write to save his life, but one of the things I'm most proud about is that my dad was a real straight shooter. A real straight shooter, down to earth, a funny guy. And I think I have those qualities.

In retrospect, how do you feel about having spent your life so far away from your parents?

There's a part of me that wishes I'd stayed in Boston to spend more time with them. That was one of the saddest things about this period of time: I just didn't understand that it was going to be happening so soon. I thought Dad would live to be a hundred, like his mother.

It's a real trade-off. I could not have made any other decision. I had to get out of there to figure out who I was and to get away from them, but it wasn't without great sacrifice.

I moved to the West Coast and started kind of a new family. It's a hard thing to do, but it seems that more and more people do it. My parents didn't move far from their parents. I think a lot about the support they had from my grandparents; I took that for granted and assumed they'd always be around. I regret that.

At the *Tin House* Summer Writers Workshops, you participated in a panel about memoir. The brochure's write-up asked, "Has our understanding of truth become too flexible or are these liberties essential for

the craft to excel as art?" Did that discussion take you anywhere unexpected? Where did you stand on the matter?

Where did I stand? Tony Swofford was talking about recreating dialogue. He felt that you could take license with that. And I thought, *Tony is so smart. Yeah, I guess you can.*

Now as I read through my book at various times, I think, *Was that verbatim? Or did I take a section of dialogue from one place and put it in another?* I was trying to be very true to what was happening, but it's possible. And I think Tony's right: you have to be able to take some liberties. I don't think you can make up conversations, but you can maybe use sections of them. Also, things are filtered through memory, and you have to honor that.

There's a passage in *The Things Between Us* where you recognize that you and your siblings have such different memories of the same events.

And completely different interpretations of what they meant. The same event can inspire all sorts of different interpretations.

My mother just died in February, and we were back there for a couple weeks during that time. It finally dawned on me why we had such different perspectives on this: they were older, seven and nine years older than I am, and they knew Mother when she was whole. They always looked at her through the eyes of loss. For me, by the time I arrived, she was pretty far gone, so I was just ecstatic to find any kind of normalcy in that environment.

Before you became an editor, you worked at Tufts in the Department of Psychology. How did you wind up in the sciences?

I studied biology and chemistry in college. I wanted to be a doctor or veterinarian. I wanted to be somebody important and serious.

I think I did that for my father. I was frightened of doing anything else. I had two examples: my father, who was sane and interested in science, and my mother, who was insane, and she was the singer and the painter and the writer. So I studied biochemistry.

I came here to Oregon and worked at OHSU. That was my first job. And I had a couple of jobs in Boston; I worked at Harvard and at Tufts. I was always trying to leave, but I had no idea what to do. I had spent so much time stuffed up, trying not to break out. I think there's some kind of process that happens when you grow up with a drunk: you don't trust yourself, you don't trust your instincts. I was trying to do something that wasn't quite right for me.

Eventually you left for the chance to get a job at an English-language magazine in Paris.

My boyfriend, whom I later married, had moved to France. I chased him. And that's where my life began to change. I had an inkling that I wanted to write. I had a lot of encouragement in writing in high school. People liked my letters, things like that. But that's where I received my education in literature, through my husband-to-be. We walked around Paris and I read many books.

When I was in high school, I read whatever it is you read,

but I didn't take English courses in college. No interest. I was going to be a serious scientist. Then I discovered this new world.

What are you reading lately? Is there a writer that continually blows you away?

I've been reading Joan Didion's novels, *Democracy* and *Play It as It Lays*. She's very interesting. As a journalist and a non-fiction writer, you'd think she would be wed to linear narrative, but her novels are so oddly structured. I've also been reading Chris Kraus: *I Love Dick*. It's a pretty amazing book.

I feel like I'm so traditional. And I really show my education at Iowa, but those people, my teachers: Deborah Eisenberg and Denis Johnson. And Charlie D'Ambrosio wasn't a teacher of mine, but I'm a huge fan of his work. Michael Ondaatje has always been a favorite of mine, as well. I thought it was very funny that at the workshops he couldn't remember parts of his book. That was great. I could see that happening, easily.

At his reading at Reed he talked about how he revises. He writes longhand, so each revision he writes out all over again. A long time ago, he did an interview that we published in the *Santa Monica Review,* and one of the things he said that really helped me, impressed me, and made a difference in my own writing, was that he worked as a poet, like a poet. He would not write chronologically. He would write all over a book. He would start with a scene and, as a poet would, put pages in a drawer every day. Eventually he would have a book.

At the time, I thought you were supposed to start at the

beginning. No. So now I write all over a book. That's how I wrote this book. Longhand scenes, and then you have to start stapling pages together. That's a very important part.

The stapler as a key tool of prose writers.

To rewrite final drafts, it's the computer, definitely. But for me the main work needs to be done longhand. That tearing apart and rearranging is important.

READING GROUP GUIDE
THE THINGS BETWEEN US
BY LEE MONTGOMERY

Discussion Points

1. Considering that this book focuses primarily on her relationship with her father, why does the author begin with: "First things first. You have to meet my mother." What does this first scene tell you about "Mumzy" and the Montgomerys' relationship? How does their behavior throughout the book reinforce your early impressions of them? Does either of them ever change? Does the way that Lee relates to them ever change?

2. Lee spent most of her childhood trying to cope with her mother and adoring her father. Why do you think Lee identifies so strongly with Big Dad? In what ways are they alike? How are they different?

3. Despite hints of a deep resentment and long-held anger, Lee still seems to love her mother very much. What is it about Barbara that Lee admires? Knowing some of the facts of her life, can you sympathize with Barbara at all?

4. Compare and contrast the author's childhood in New England with her adulthood in Southern California and

Oregon. In what ways do the two regions offer similar experiences? In what ways are they different?

5. On page 7, Lee calls her father a "classic Yankee." Using examples from the book, explain what she means by this.

6. Lee and her father "spend [their] lives together doing chores," (pp. 14–15). Even after she moves away, they complete projects together over the phone. What is the symbolism inherent in this characterization? What does it tell you about their respective roles in the family?

7. The author describes her mother's family, the Begoles, as a family that "loses things." What has Barbara Begole Montgomery lost? Do you think Lee is a part of that legacy? If so, what has *she* lost? What is she trying to find?

8. On pages 4–8, Lee describes her family as planets in the solar system. Why does she make each of her associations between family members and their respective orbiting masses?

9. When you think of a "New England WASP," what comes to mind? How do the Montgomerys hold up to your stereotype?

10. Sprinkled throughout this memoir are moments of violence or extreme emotional reaction, mostly the result of days, months, and sometimes years of repression. Identify each of these moments and discuss how they reveal the private struggles of the people involved.

11. The author spends a lot of time describing Big Dad's hands as she moves with him through the final months of his life. Discuss the appearance and significance of hands and the ways the author uses them as a symbol.

12. The three Montgomery children each sped away from

their childhood and its memories as soon as they were able. Yet, as their father declines, they spend a lot of time recollecting their lives at Four Corner Farm. What changes do you see happening to them and between them, due to revisiting these memories?

13. Lee, in particular, obsesses about her relationships with her parents and siblings, who have left her feeling disconnected and abandoned for different reasons over the years. Discuss her conflicting needs to be both close and distant from her family at various points in her life.

14. *The Things Between Us* explores the dying "blueblood" New England lifestyle, thus providing a fascinating window into an American subculture on the wane. What is the town of Framingham, Massachusetts, like? In what ways is the Montgomerys' world just like any American family's? In what ways is it different?

15. Many authors write memoirs in order to better deal with their painful experiences. In detailing his life and death, how has Lee Montgomery paid homage to her father? What do you think about her portrayal of her mother, considering the facts of their history together? What clues do you see in *The Things Between Us* that reveal how the author has or hasn't been able to come to terms with her family's love- and resentment-filled past?

Enhance Your Book Club Experience

Research the Boston, Massachusetts area and the small community of Framingham. You can start with information and photos at *www.visitnewengland.com* and *http://www.visit-massachusetts.com/boston.html*. Have a "Yankee" party and go horseback riding, apple-picking, drink cocktails, and share what you've learned of the region's history. You can even have everyone prepare and bring New England foods, such as those found at *www.newenglandrecipes.com*. Learn about the ongoing foxhunting tradition (though of course they don't use real foxes anymore) that's carried on by the Old North Bridge Hounds at *www.onbh.org*—you may even be able to follow one of their hunts.

As a group or individually, watch the movies *War of the Roses* (which the Montgomerys found hysterically funny) and *When a Man Loves a Woman* (a movie about the struggle a husband and child face in the wake of one woman's alcoholism). Discuss the effects of alcoholism on all the Montgomerys, parents and children alike.

For more information on the book or Lee Montgomery, visit *www.TheThingsBetweenUs.com*